Peggy's Cove

The Amazing History
of a Coastal Village

Lesley Choyce

Pottersfield Press, Lawrencetown Beach, Nova Scotia, Canada

Library and Archives Canada Cataloguing in Publication

Choyce,Lesley, 1951-
    Peggy's Cove : the amazing history of a coastal village / Lesley Choyce.

ISBN 978-1-897426-00-5

1. Peggys Cove (N.S.) – History. 2. Peggys Cove (N.S.) – Description and travel. I. Title.

FC2349.P45C46 2008   971.6'22   C2008-903164-4

Cover design by Gail LeBlanc

Cover photo: istockphoto

The author would like to thank Michelle Mulder for her research assistance as well as Peggy Amirault and Julia Swan for their diligence in editorial work.

Pottersfield Press acknowledges the financial support of the Government of Canada through the Book Publishing Industry Development Program for our publishing activities. We acknowledge the ongoing support of the Canada Council for the Arts, which last year invested $20.1 million in writing and publishing throughout Canada. We also thank the Province of Nova Scotia for its support through the Department of Tourism, Culture and Heritage.

Pottersfield Press
83 Leslie Road
East Lawrencetown, Nova Scotia, Canada, B2Z 1P8
Website: www.pottersfieldpress.com
To order phone toll-free 1-800-NIMBUS9 (1-800-646-2879)
Printed in Canada

To the People of Peggy's Cove –
Past and Present

Contents

Introduction

Waves of White and Blue Ferocity

A wave crashes ashore at Peggy's Cove.

The parking lot by the Sou'Wester Restaurant near the Peggy's Point lighthouse is empty on a bitterly cold January morning. The sun is low in the east and waves left over from a nor'easter are pounding the rocky shores with the sound of cannons. As I walk the path towards the lighthouse, I see spiralling threads of mist rising from the ocean. Sea smoke or sea wraiths are the result of very cold air over the relatively warmer water. The sun filters through these dancing ghosts and makes the whole scene surreal.

The rocks are giant round, smooth monuments that seem to have been sculpted by the hands of artists. There is an impossible, otherworldly haunting quality to this place. The battery of waves continues in surround sound. Gulls are rising and dipping in the chill winter air.

My own thoughts are pure. I am overwhelmed by this place. I've been here before many times but now, alone like this, I give in to a feeling of reverence resulting from the stark, hard beauty I see before me. The sweep of the bare granite seacoast stretches for miles to the east. I look down at where I walk, wary of the patchy ice – seawater that has frozen on these massive stones.

The powerful waves from yesterday's storm – now headed north and east towards Newfoundland – rear up with white and blue ferocity and then slam with all their might into the massive walled rocks. Close up, the crashing wave has a different sound now, that of an uncontrolled explosion, and it is followed by the spewing white foamy spray rocketing two storeys into the air. I cautiously study the rock beneath my feet and stand only where it is dry. I am mesmerized as each wave in a set of ten tries to outdo the previous one with its intensity.

I hunker down in a safe place beneath a rocky outcropping, far enough from the danger of exploding waves to prevent myself from being pummelled and sucked into the maw of the raging sea, but close enough to draw upon the intense energy of the great salty show before me. The waves come in sets of seven to ten with a minute or two respite between.

The sun is full upon my face and has lit up the landscape around me with rich morning tones of yellow, copper and rust colours. It feels like a sacred moment and I am reminded that the early inhabitants of Nova Scotia, the Mi'kmaq people, knew this place and made pilgrimages here to feel just what I am feeling now: awe of the natural beauty and power and the awareness of being in the presence of larger forces. It might be enough to say that those forces are the elements themselves. The North Atlantic, the sun rising up out of the sea, the swooping gulls, the massive waves. But it is more than that as well. There is a spiritual presence here that I do not quite have a name for. I'm sure the Mi'kmaq had a word for it, however, and others who have visited here may have also named it.

Standing up now with the flood of light and the leaping spray of waves catching that morning sun to deliver a shower of crystals, I feel both small and large. Small, because I feel in my bones how insignificant I am in the presence of such grandeur and power. Large, because I feel intrinsically connected to all this rock and sea and sky. Beyond the crashing waves, the Atlantic stretches out in its immensity from here to Europe, from here to Morocco. I am reminded that these boulders beneath me were once part of what is now the northwest corner of that continent. I am positioned on what was once a part of Africa.

Alone on the shore here at Peggy's Cove, there is nothing in my immediate vision that is of this century or any of the previous hundred. I have travelled back in time and am a mere tourist in a world of ancient cold seas and antediluvian geology. It is humbling and profound. I feel the hair on the back of my neck stand up.

And I feel that other presence: of God, of spirit, of things larger and unknown. I wonder what it was like for those first Europeans who sailed past here and for those who had the courage to guide their boats into the little harbour and step ashore. Did they see it as a wasteland? For on one level, there is nothing here.

It is the emptiness and barrenness of Peggy's Cove and the surrounding hills that give an unearthly quality. And yet, it is one of the wonders of the world. Millions have made pilgrimage here, not exactly knowing why. Most would be called tourists, yes. Most don't venture too far from the restaurant and the parking lot, maybe a walk to the lighthouse and back. (And even that short walk has at times been fraught with danger.) But most go away having been touched in some deep and elemental way by Peggy's Cove and by the forces at work here.

The other thing you realize in the most primitive part of yourself, alone here on the frosty morning, is how dangerous this place can be. If I were to walk four steps forward, still standing on solid horizontal rock – if I were to move there right now and just wait – a wave would arrive that would crash into the rock face before me, vault into the air like an icy demon, then crash down with a good ton of water from above, pull me from where I stand and drag me into the depths below, where I would be pounded against the shoreline by its next brother to follow.

You can't help but think about that as you stare it all down – the beauty, the spirit, the barren geography and the danger. Tragically, some have died here, ships foundering on the ledges beyond and tourists swept from the rocks, not quite willing to believe that those warning signs are serious business.

Peggy's Cove, more than most places I know, is a focal point of life and of death. And therein lies a story. A story of one of the most unique places on earth. A story about these bare rocks, the glaciers that scraped them clean, the sea that sculpted them and then the people who chose to live here. And the joys and sorrows that followed.

1

A Gift from Africa

A stark and beautiful landscape resulting from glacial activity.

Some of us fall in love with those rocks at Peggy's Cove. Their beauty and grandeur represent something ancient and elemental, there is no doubt. But these rocks were not always here. They migrated from a great distance.

Far away in what would be today the other side of the Atlantic, deposits of sand and mud became compacted beneath the ocean and eventually helped form the coastline of the ancient continent of Gondwana. This took place nearly 500 million years ago. Then the sand and mud became compressed, forming shale and sandstone. The climate above the land and sea then would have been quite hot there near the earth's equator.

A mere 400 million years ago a collision occurred. Gondwana crashed (ever so slowly) into what was the formative continent of North America as the crustal plates of the earth shifted, creating massive impacts. The heat and pressure of the event changed the softer rock into harder substances, primarily slate and quartzite. At the lower levels of this earth-shaking event, the heat melted the material, it spewed upward as lava and then cooled into granite.

Peggy's Cove, 350 million years ago and then near the equator, was still "recovering" from the intercontinental collision. There were mountains and valleys formed and the sea spilled into one of those valleys, creating what is now St. Margaret's Bay. After about another fifty million years, the continents pulled apart. The map of the earth continued to change and, as Gondwana moved east and south, rock was dragged and dropped along the way, making for the ragged, rugged coastline Nova Scotia is famous for. What was left jammed into North America was essentially once part of Africa.

The rock that is here today is of the same substance as that to be found in Morocco if you were to go there and dig beneath the sands. Here on the Atlantic shore, the granite formed the backbone of this place and remains a fixed memory of our African geological heritage. There is a fault line that runs through Nova Scotia from the Bay of Fundy to Chedabucto Bay. Most of what is on the south and west side of that line are the remains of Gondwana and that includes the great boulders of Peggy's Cove.

Long after that, a mere million years ago, the ice advanced south and covered Nova Scotia in a sheet that was one and a half kilometres thick. Five or six times the ice sheet advanced and retreated. During the warmer phases, life would develop. At other times, the ice cover would be as thick as four kilometres, smothering everything beneath and pushing the land downward.

The last retreat of ice was probably 10,000 years ago and what remained was a scarred and ravaged land. Most of the soil and surface materials had been pushed southward, much of it deposited in what is today the Grand Banks. There the sediment helped create what would be the greatest fishing ground in the world. The bedrock left behind was both shaped and polished by the sand and ice in the retreat. This gave us the curved and elaborate shapes of the rocks of Peggy's Cove. The retreat also left gouges in the land which became lakes, most of them etched in a north-south direction. Great deposits of sediment were left as well in cigar-shaped hills along the coast that formed drumlins. Today, most coastal drumlins are partially eroded, but what remains of these soft-shouldered hills can still be seen along the South and Eastern Shores.

The work of the glaciers also left Nova Scotia with moraines (piles of loose glacial till), kettle holes and other reminders of the massive impact of the ice. After the glaciers departed, the land rebounded, rising up like dough as it was freed from the profound weight of ice. At the same time, the melting ice made the seas rise dramatically, flooding the lowlands and valleys and forging inlets landward to merge salt and fresh water.

Even as the departing ice scoured the stone, rocks stuck in the moving ice cut grooves and gouges in even the hardest surfaces. You can see these marks today in places where the sea has not continued to polish the stone. Usually the marks will be in a north-south direction.

After the ice was gone, soil began to form from the sediment left and from the decay of plants but in places like the Cove where bedrock was close to the shoreline, it remained bare and exposed with only small deposits of silt and very specialized life forms taking hold.

Some of those glacially carved rocks around Peggy's Cove have been given names over the years for their unique shape, history and personality. The Whalesback is inland about one and a half kilometres from the community and

The granite rocks, weathered and cracked by time and the elements.

a restaurant bears its name. There is also Halibut Rock by the lighthouse (possibly where the legendary Peggy was shipwrecked), Dancing Rock, where picnics and dances once took place, Black Rock, Five Alley Rock, Simon's Rock, the Devil's Armchair and others.

Clearly, Peggy's Cove would not have the fame it has today had it not been carved by the glaciers and had it not become home to these great granite stones.

Far off the shores of Peggy's Cove, the Grand Banks became a great breeding ground for fish, especially cod. There the Labrador Current, 400 metres deep and 350 kilometres wide, sweeps down from the north with rich nutrients and minute sea creatures. The Labrador collides with the Gulf Stream, 400 to 800 kilometres off Nova Scotia, creating a dynamic breeding ground for plankton and small fishes that provide sustenance for the bigger fish. In years past, the omnivorous codfish could grow to be ninety-six kilograms. Today, the cod stocks have declined to what some fear may lead to extinction. The history of fishing in Nova Scotia played a significant role in the life of the people of the Cove down through the years, although it is much diminished today.

It's possible that 6,000 years ago much of Nova Scotia looked like the rocks of Peggy's Cove – barren and starkly beautiful. Today, the boulders of the Cove appear as if it was just a short time ago that glaciers covered this land and they remind us that, someday, the arctic ice may return.

Dinosaurs and, later, mastodons wandered around Nova Scotia and may have visited the shores here. Concrete evidence is found in parts of the province in the form of fossilized remains.

For centuries there has been a rich abundance of fish close to the shores of Peggy's Cove. The plant life that survives today in and around the rocks is highly specialized and uniquely adapted to these conditions. The land and waterways nearby supported wildlife in the form of beaver, muskrat, otter, ermine, red fox, black bear, caribou, and white-tailed deer, to name a few. Many of this natural population are now absent or dramatically reduced from days gone by. In the skies overhead soared bald eagles, osprey and red-tailed hawks. Gulls, ravens and crows were everpresent and still seem to be at home among the throngs of visitors. Many types of salt and freshwater waterfowl have been documented in and around Peggy's Cove over the years.

The first humans most likely to have lived along the shores here are the Mi'kmaq. Coming from homes farther inland, they would come here in the summers to harvest fish and hunt. Arrowheads have been found at several locations around St. Margaret's Bay and the name of at least one Mi'kmaq family is recorded on a land grant of the 1700s. The Mi'kmaq wisely retreated to the inland forests of the South Shore in the winter to avoid the ravages of storms near the sea.

Since the traditional Mi'kmaq religion was based on a personal and spiritual kinship to the natural world around them, they must have found Peggy's Cove to be a powerful and sacred place. Not long ago, while visiting, I came across a former Mi'kmaq university student of mine with children from a summer camp collecting sweet grass from the nearby marshes, which would later be burned as part of an ancient ceremony honouring ancestors and the land.

2

First Families and Foundering Ships

Ships in Halifax Harbour circa 1752 as the Foreign Protestants were arriving.

Samuel de Champlain sailed along this coast on his first voyage to Acadia in 1604. He gets credit for the first European record of the Peggy's Cove area, naming the bay for his mother, Margarite, and later raising his mother to sainthood status in his map of 1612 with the label as St. Margarite Baie.

No French settled this corner of Acadia, however, instead finding Port Royal on the Bay of Fundy more suitable for a permanent settlement. The English focused on settling along the shores of Halifax Harbour but between 1749 and 1752 decided to lure "Foreign Protestants" to come to Nova Scotia to settle on the South Shore, particularly around Lunenburg.

The British government wanted Protestants under fifty years of age who would be loyal to the king but could not find enough of its own citizens volunteering for the task of creating new towns. So it enticed continental Europeans, trying to avoid war, persecution and starvation, to sail across the Atlantic. Each family was promised a fifty-acre land grant, food and implements. The immigrants came from southern Germany, Switzerland and Holland and suf-

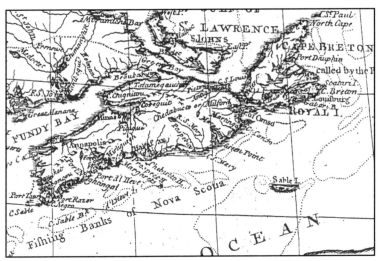

An English map of Nova Scotia, 1750.

fered severely on the trip over due to the greed and corruption of the shipowners.

The immigration agents were paid a fee for each passenger so they crammed the ships for the dangerous nine-to-thirteen-week voyage. In many instances, the water was bad and the food rotten. Many became sick and died along the way. Upon arrival, the immigrants were told they would have to work at hard labour in Halifax to pay for the cost of their transport to Nova Scotia before being allowed to get on with a new life on the South Shore. It wasn't until a rebellion nearly broke out that the military guided them to Lunenburg and land grants were issued. By 1753, 1,600 Foreign Protestants had settled in Lunenburg, and, along with several English families, some began to settle around St. Margaret's Bay.

The first family known to settle in Peggy's Cove was William Rodgers and his wife, Margaret, but after living there for six years, they moved on to Caribou Island near Pictou. Other families of Foreign Protestant descent found life in the rugged cove preferable to "town" life in Lunenburg and "city" life in Halifax. There must have been plenty of elbow room for everyone since a poll of the citizens all around St. Margaret's Bay in 1759 noted a whopping total of forty-nine families. Clearly, there was enough farmland and fishing to supply everyone's needs.

Originally known as Eastern Point Harbour, the 800-acre parcel of land around the Cove was divided up in 1811 among six families of German descent: brothers George, William and John Isenhauer (Isnor); John Kayzer; and William and George Troop (Troup). This was an outright land grant from King George III signed by Sir George Prevost, the designated baronet of this part of Nova Scotia. These families were granted the following:

> ... the Fish Rooms stages and pasture grounds they occupy cultivate and improve containing eight hundred acres of land situate lying and being at Margaret's Bay aforesaid and comprehended within the following limits beginning at the southern bound of land formerly granted Foster Sherlock on the eastern shore near the entrance to Margaret's Bay thence to run north sixty-eight degrees east ninety-eight chains along the line of said Sherlock's land thence south twenty-two degrees east one hundred and twenty chains

thence south twenty-two degrees west eighty
chains or until it comes to the sea shore
thence northerly by the several courses of the
shore until it meets the place of beginning.

These lots would later be divided into twenty-five. It's
hard to say why these families found themselves owning
this particular corner of the world except to observe that
the tiny cove itself was deep and sheltered and it would
be a good place to fish. Farming would certainly not be
easy anywhere near the shore. As generations would come
to recognize, it would be considerably foggier and damper
at Peggy's Cove than most places along the South Shore,
and being located by the open sea would mean greater impact from storms and more dangerous fishing conditions. It
would be safe to say that only the most stalwart and robust
of settlers would remain at the Cove and call it home. The
riches of the sea were at their doorstep, but the personal
price to pay for harvesting from the sea was steep.

These first families of the Cove were later joined by immigrants of Irish, Scottish and English descent. "Only the
good Lord knows why," said Lawson Innis, a lifelong resident of Peggy's Cove in an interview in 1947.

There are three versions (possibly more) about how the
area got its name. The more mundane version is simply
that Peggy's Cove is situated at the entrance to St. Margaret's Bay and so it was shortened to the nickname, Peggy.
The second version suggests that the Cove was named for
the wife of the early Irish resident, William Rodgers, who
may have named the place but still found the living tough
enough to prompt him to move himself and his family to a

less severe locale if he wanted to save his marriage.

A favoured and more romantic story states that a schooner foundered on the rocks near where the lighthouse is today (Halibut Rock). It was a stormy October night with strong southeast winds bringing sleet and fog. All on board were tumbled into the sea and lost except for one woman named Margaret. She clambered ashore and clung to the slippery rocks, eventually pulling herself up to safety. For unknown reasons, she decided to live in the tiny cove community. Perhaps she was simply determined never to go to sea again. She married a local man and she liked to tell stories. Folks from nearby villages came to visit and were entertained by her tales. They called her "Peggy of the Cove," which later led to the village itself being called Peggy's Cove.

In Ivan Fraser's 2004 book, *Peggy of the Cove*, he embellishes the story, which he calls a "legend brought to reality." In his tale, Peggy is only eight years old at the time of the shipwreck. Whether there is any truth to the tale is hard to say. It seems to have become accepted when it appeared in print in William E. deGarthe's 1956 book, *This is Peggy's Cove, Nova Scotia*. It may have just been a good yarn making the rounds since deGarthe admits, "How true this story is, no one knows, and there are no documents available to confirm or refute it." But what the heck, it's a good story and we all seem to wish there was a real Peggy back there in the mists of Cove history – whether she was legend or fact.

Bruce Nunn, known as Mr. Nova Scotia Know-It-All, however, says that he spoke with a woman in California who claims to be the real Peggy's great-granddaughter.

Margaret Maxine Roeper (formerly Miller) was in her seventies and claimed that her great-grannie was so young she didn't even know her name when she washed ashore in the Cove. She was adopted and raised by a family named Weaver and, when she grew up, moved to North Dakota.

Whatever the truth, the spirit of Peggy lives on at the Cove and surfaces from year to year as fiction, poetry, art and drama. Immortality by any other name could never be as sweet.

3

The Pious and the Privateers

The captured American warship **Chesapeake** *in Nova Scotia waters, 1813.*

Down through the centuries, the residents were spared the immediate horrors of war, although the effects of wars certainly had an impact economically and personally on everyday lives. During the War of 1812 between the British and the Americans, Yankee privateer ships hid among the islands of St. Margaret's Bay and along other inlets on the South Shore. It was impossible for the British navy to police the many bays and harbours around the province, and the enemy privateers (literally pirates legitimized by one side or the other) were free to pillage what they could from both ships at sea and communities along the coast.

The waters off the Cove had seen privateers before, although there is no record of attacks on Peggy's Cove itself. But it was not unheard of for American privateers to come ashore and trade with the locals, enterprise that was profitable for both. As in many coastal communities of the Maritimes, the law was ignored in the name of commerce that would enhance the well-being of family.

During the War of 1812, not far away in Mahone Bay, one such vessel called the *Young Teazer* was hiding after several brazen attacks on British merchant ships. Spotted by a British naval ship, she tried to make a run for the high seas and in the process, someone aboard accidentally set light to the ship's supply of dynamite. The *Young Teazer* blew up in a tremendous explosion and only eight crewmen survived. Today, people living in Mahone Bay claim they still see the "*Teazer* Light" on some nights – an inexplicable glow that moves along the water, ending in a bright burst, a paranormal remnant of the explosion.

By 1817, the population of the bay area had risen to 506. Communities developed as relatively isolated fishing villages using boats for transport from town to town. The first roads were wilderness trails filled with rocks and stumps over some very difficult terrain. The interior landscape around the Cove is much the same today as it was then, so it is not hard to imagine what land travel would be like. Local residents seemed not to care that the province had little interest in improving the land routes because they had the sea for their highway. Eventually, the government would provide grants to improve the roads locally to entice men away from their daily work on the sea or on farms.

Schooners sailed out of the bay with goods for Halifax and beyond – lumber, fish, cattle – with passengers aboard as well. On the return trip from the city, the schooners would bring manufactured goods and other supplies from the outside world.

Religious concerns were mainly family matters for the early settlers but the Church of England took an interest in bringing its faith to rural Nova Scotia and the Reverend Charles Inglis, Canada's first Bishop of the Church of Canada, carved out a parish from Boutilier's Point to Timberlea to Bayside that was called St. Paul's Mission. He reportedly travelled to St. Margaret's Bay on occasion and discussed religious concerns with area inhabitants.

In the early 1800s, Peggy's Cove citizens had set aside land for a church but it seems they didn't get around to building it. It was much like the road situation, I suppose. Feed your family first and worry about other stuff if there is any daylight left. They never did build a church there but used the land for a schoolhouse instead, later in 1839. The church was the authority for education, after all, so this is not as blasphemous as it sounds. In 1823, Peggy's Cove had its own school district. The parents funded the teachers and the running of the school, although the teacher was usually selected by the church and almost certainly would be of the same denomination.

Anglican teachers must have been hard to come by, however, because Reverend John Stannage, the first pastor of the Peggy's Cove congregation from 1834 to 1856, received some flack from the local Protestants by hiring at least one teacher of the Catholic faith. During those times prejudice still ran deep between Protestant and Catholic, much of it anchored in the political wrangling between the British and the French.

Over the years, religious differences were set aside, but the 1839 school is still standing. It was in use right up until 1958, 119 years later, which I guess says something about the population growth of the Cove area.

The great Nova Scotia writer, rambler and politician, Joseph Howe, visited Peggy's Cove in 1839 and wrote, "At several settlements along the line of coast stretching between Halifax and the Bay, the people have no other resources but the fishery, for there is so little soil scattered over the granite rock upon which they reside, that sufficient is scarcely found in some places to make a cabbage garden." Nonetheless, many Cove residents made do with what soil existed in pockets between the boulders and they grew family gardens of cabbages, potatoes, turnip and other staples. Hay was grown in broader patches of low-lying ground that would be at least partially rock-free.

A bit inland, some of the fields supported significant crops of hay grown for the livestock. Cutting would begin early in the morning with razor-sharp scythes and a good man wielding that scythe could mow an acre in a day. The hay would be piled into the proverbial haystacks and pitchforked apart the next morning to dry. Then later that day it would be stored away to last into the winter months.

Eelgrass grew in the shallow water along the shores nearby and was harvested as it washed up along the shoreline. It was a valuable resource for most coastal Nova Scotians as it was used to mulch gardens and also for insulating houses, stuffing pillows and packing glass. In some parts of the province, eelgrass was harvested and shipped off to the States for profit.

Joe Howe must have liked Peggy's Cove, because he returned there several times and on one occasion had this to say:

> We were down at Peggy's Cove a few weeks ago, and while sitting at tea, were informed that there was a fiddler in a neighboring house, and that the young people were going to have a dance. We went to the place,

and I never saw a finer lot of young men and women. I took off my coat and danced with them, and a most cheerful night was passed, without impropriety or excess. Towards twelve o'clock it was pleasant to see how each young fisherman's arm found its way round his sweetheart's neck, and thus the scene passed on, cheerfully and innocent.

There is a clear idyllic sound to his rendering and it may have created a sharp contrast to life then in Halifax, a city with hard drinking and fist-fighting nightly at the many taverns and brothels. Howe did tend to romanticize Nova Scotians in rural communities and outports, but it's good to hear one of the most intelligent men of that era finding the upbeat side of life in the isolated little village, where much of human existence would, of necessity, be hard and often dangerous.

In 1848 it was recorded that the Cove had nineteen "boys" ranging in age from six to twenty-three and only thirteen "girls" aged seven to fifteen. In the little school where many of them were being educated, they studied spelling, English, geography, arithmetic and the Bible.

Land travel began to improve mid-century as a stage-coach line went into operation when the Royal Western Mail Shore Line began biweekly journeys from Halifax to Lunenburg and back. With a bit of an overland trek, the folks from Peggy's Cove could now access a bumpy ride to Halifax should they decide that weather made the sea voyage too deadly. The Shore Line kept its horses in harness up until 1904, when the Halifax and Southwestern Railway came into being.

Reverend John Stannage, originally from New Jersey, had been overseeing religious matters in the neighbourhood for more than a decade when he held a public meeting in December of 1847 and he convinced the community it was time to build a chapel. Although he had a few detractors, most of the local citizens were behind him. Stannage was able to raise money from outside as well. Some well-to-do Halifax businessmen donated funds as did the Honourable H.H. Cogswell and J. Inglis Haliburton. A local man, James Croucher, perhaps hopeful of keeping his family closer to God than most, donated the land alongside of his own home and the small St. John's Chapel was completed in 1850.

4

Lobsters, Cod and Sea Serpents

Loading the **Francis Robie.**

Fish had been crucial to the survival of the people of the Cove from the very beginning. Local fishermen never had to venture very far from their wharves for a reasonable catch. Cod, mackerel, haddock, herring, sole, and pollack were plentiful and there was an abundance of lobster.

Lobsters were a significant source of food for the first residents, the Mi'kmaq, who called them *wolum keeh*. It is believed they were so abundant that they could just be plucked from the shallows or collected from the exposed seaweed at low tide. The earliest white settlers probably hooked them with gaffs from boats not far from shore. In some parts of Nova Scotia, men went out on the water on calm nights with torches to locate the crustaceans and then spear them and haul them into the boat. Another method was to drop cod heads into the cold, clear water to attract the lobsters and then catch them with the spear or gaff.

Although we consider lobster a delicacy today, in Nova Scotia in the nineteenth century, it was strictly seen as a "poor man's food." Families along the coast here could feast often on the delectable abundant lobster during much of the year. When it became more of a commercial commodity, spearing (which left wounds in the shell) was replaced by the lobster trap made from a frame of wood and fish net. Fishermen would row their dories out to sea in the very early morning hours and set the traps, returning the next day to remove the lobsters and reset the traps again. Fortunately for the men of the Cove, they never had to row very far from home for their catch.

If the lobster was sold to the fish packers, the fishermen were paid, not by the pound, but by the number of lobsters. Forty to fifty cents for one hundred lobsters was considered a fair price.

Some families along the coasts of Nova Scotia attempted to can their own lobster for use out of season or for sale to buyers. The lobsters were boiled and the meat was extracted, then packed in tins and a lid sealed with lead solder. Saltwater would be forced into the can through a hole and then that would be soldered as well. It was an imperfect process at best, leading to a lot of rotten lobster meat that must have smelled horrendous upon opening the can. As some put it, the lobster was "green in the sea, red in the pot and black in the can." Suffice it to say, this method of preservation eventually faded from use.

A bit farther out from shore could be found tuna, although it was not very popular among shore dwellers as it was considered an inferior fish. Tuna were called "horse mackerel" by the fishermen because they had large eyes and a head with some resemblance to a horse's head. Around St. Margaret's Bay, tuna was sometimes referred to as "sea lion," probably because of its considerable size. It wasn't until later in 1903 when locals were alerted to the demand for tuna from Italian immigrants in Boston that fishermen became a bit more serious about harvesting this species and shipping it south.

After that, tuna became more popular as part of the local menu for the people of Peggy's Cove. But it was a fishery somewhat more dangerous than that of cod or mackerel. The tuna were big, the boats were small and the tuna could not be easily caught using nets. Catching tuna with a hook and line was very risky. Spears were used and a genuine fight ensued that cost more than one fisherman his life. Once aboard the small boats, tuna would be killed with an axe if necessary. Clearly, it was a perilous, bloody business that made more than one fishermen wish he was hoisting nets of harmless herring rather than testing his stamina against these noble lions of the sea.

Swordfishing came into the picture later as that fish also proved to fetch a high price when sent to market. But, like tuna fishing, it was more hazardous as a man must harness himself to his boat, haul in the great beast weighing six or seven hundred pounds and again slay the great sea creature with its dangerous sword using whatever bloody means was available.

Cod, on the other hand, had always been a staple of the folks along the shores of Nova Scotia and Newfoundland. For centuries, European ships had come to the waters off Nova Scotia to harvest cod. John Cabot, in his early explorations of this region in the fifteenth century, noted an "immense quantity of fish." He wrote that all that was necessary was to dip baskets over the side to pull up the catch and that on at least one occasion, the cod were so thick in the North Atlantic where he sailed that they impeded the progress of his vessel.

However, as we grew to learn, the cod is a sensitive breed. Over-harvesting and changes in water temperature could drastically reduce or destroy the stock. As early as 1739, one expert on fish of that day reported of the cod, "There has not been the slightest appearance of fish stock this fall. This has greatly astonished our fishermen – who will all be wiped out." If the cod had gone away, they eventually came back and continued to be harvested in massive quantities right up into the 1980s, when it became clear that the cod was over-fished and disappearing.

But in the 1800s, the cod was still plentiful and relatively "easy" to catch. The handlines with many baited hooks were dropped over the side from a boat – often in the fall. Within two hours, a Peggy's Cove inshore fisherman might have had twenty or thirty fish, weighing in at twenty pounds or more each. The cod would be eaten fresh or salted for the winter.

Cod caught in the spring was dried in the sun – should there be enough days without rain or heavy fog – on wooden lathes set up on poles known as "flakes." Once dried by the sun and air, it was stored for later consumption or sold to markets in Halifax, Boston, Europe and the Caribbean.

Much of the fishing done over the side of boats involved handmade nets. The mesh would vary according to the size of fish being caught. The nets were made with cotton twine woven with wooden or bone needles or sometimes store-bought needles made from brass. Men, women and young boys made the nets. Sometimes the whole family pitched in to support the father who took his boat to sea for their livelihood. In order to camouflage and protect the nets from algae growth and rot, they were soaked in a tanning solution made from spruce buds collected in the spring. The new nets were immersed in boiling water containing the spruce and boiled for fifteen minutes, at which point the cotton had turned a brownish-purple colour that made it somewhat invisible underwater to the fish.

Usually the nets, if they were still intact and reusable at the end of a season, were repaired and resoaked for the next round of use. The spruce preservative method was later replaced by a resin known as "cutch" (catechu) that came from Asia and was bought from local dealers. Into the 1930s and beyond many were still making nets by hand, although factory-made products were available.

The nets used by traditional fishermen of these shores did eventually disintegrate and needed replacement but even if they were lost at sea, they would tend to sink and decay. And that was a good thing. Today, large synthetic nets are designed to be nearly indestructible and when they are lost at sea – in all the world's oceans – they drift for days, weeks or even years, catching fish and killing them needlessly and in vast numbers. As they often say, the old ways are sometimes the best ways. And when it comes to a sensible harvest of the fish from a once-generous sea, that is certainly true of traditional inshore fishing in Nova Scotia.

In 1850, John Crooks opened a general store not far from the water's edge, and it became a social hub as well as the focus of local commerce. The store carried everyday household items as well as goods needed by fishermen. Men would gather there to smoke and discuss the catch of the day, politics and, invariably, the weather. The store remained on its original property until a sinister storm in 1898 flooded the community, lifting the building and moving it across the road. Part of the store was left hanging over the water and in order to salvage what was usable, it was cut in two and ended up being half of its original size.

The hardy residents of Peggy's Cove grew up observing many curious, unusual and sometimes frightening surprises offered up by the ever-changing ocean. Perhaps most astonishing was the sighting of sea monsters – creatures even more daunting than the tuna and swordfish that were fished off these shores. The first recorded sighting of a "sea serpent" in St. Margaret's Bay was in 1833 by three soldiers from the British Rifle Brigade who were out on a fishing trip. In 1846, the same serpent (or its look-alike cousin) appeared right at Peggy's Cove and was reported by James Wilson and John Boehner. Corroborating their story was George Dauphinee, who said he saw the beast nearby in Hackett's Cove.

Down through the ages, sailors on all the world's oceans had reported seeing frightening sea creatures of many sorts. One of the most famous was the Kraken, spotted off the coast of Greenland in 1734. A sailor reported, "The monster was so huge in size that, coming out of the water, its head reached as high as a mainmast; its body was as bulky as a ship, and three or four times as long." The long tentacles of a giant squid or octopus were often thought to be serpents as well. One such creature was caught off the coast of Newfoundland in 1878 with a body twenty feet long and thirty-five-foot-long tentacles.

Nothing of such grand proportions was ever seen in Peggy's Cove but there were some very strange-looking and unidentifiable fish that had been landed over the years. And many remained on the lookout for that bizarre creature that had surfaced in the 1830s and 1840s. The Peggy's Cove beast was as elusive as the Loch Ness monster. There were supposed sightings of the serpent or "monster," but it remained more legend than fact until the following appeared in the *Acadian Reporter* on August 5, 1872:

> A gentleman, who has just returned from St. Margaret's Bay, reported that the great sea serpent made its appearance on Saturday last, in the vicinity of Miller's and George's Islands. Something like a large barrel was observed floating in the water. A party of fishermen went out to investigate the matter. When they discovered that what they took to be a barrel was the monster's head, they were terrified, as on their approach, the terrible animal stretched its jaws disclosing a mouth of vivid red colour. The frightened men at once turned and, in haste, rowed ashore. The animal was afterwards passed by another boat, the men in which affirm that they saw at least 30 feet of this length and judged it to be considerably longer ... It is said to be destroying the poor people's nets, going through them and rending them at its pleasure. It is also averred that this, or a similar sea serpent, appears in the vicinity about once every 10-15 years.

Beyond that, there was continued anecdotal evidence that something large, strange and fearsome lurks or lurked in these clear cold waters beyond the smooth boulders of the Cove. A large, unidentifiable sea creature was actually captured later in the twentieth century and in 1982 the local sea monster was declared the mascot of the St. Margaret's Bay Business and Tourism Association.

Dangers of sea monsters notwithstanding, the fishing was good for the men of the Cove in the pre-Confederation days of Nova Scotia. Peggy's Cove itself was a busy little harbour with wharves, fishing stores and stages crammed around the water and boats aplenty bobbing above the swaying rust-coloured seaweed. With free entry to New England markets, fish of many species were shipped south for reasonably good prices. Hard work was rewarded with enough pay to feed a family and keep a household. The population of Peggy's Cove was roughly 400 at one point, with most of those families living in small, modest two-storey houses that were little more than a stone's throw from the water.

By mid-century, postal service had arrived in the area and Peggy's Cove had its own postmaster, a position that would be handed down within the family. Delivery of the mail was by horse and carriage, at first three days a week. The rail line aided in delivery after that – bringing the mail to an inland station from which the postmaster would have to provide final delivery to the Cove. The postal service was quite a significant leap for the people of the area, allowing them to feel more connected with the outside world, providing regular reports of fish prices elsewhere and vital news from friends and relatives in Halifax and beyond. Wesley Crooks, still just a boy, became acting postmaster in

A simple Life, House 8×10 Mill Cove N. S.

An early postcard depicting the "simple life" of a coastal family in nearby Mill Cove.

1858 and got the official appointment as postmaster when he turned twenty-three.

A major decline in the price of fish caused hardship for the families of the Cove in the 1860s. Some families moved inland where there were jobs to be found in the forests and in the sawmills that were popping up around St. Margaret's Bay. Ever dependent on what a distant market determined was the value of cod and mackerel, the people of the Cove may have wondered if the good days were behind them. Was it possible that the "traditional" way of life by the sea would not be there for their children?

And now that news of the outside world found its way on a regular basis to their doorstep, there were other new fears that surfaced, many of them unfounded. The Fenians, an Irish-American organization committed to freeing Ireland from England, was founded in 1861. The nearest

British presence to the U.S. was of course Canada and the Fenians undertook a series of armed raids into New Brunswick across the Maine border. This raised alarms along the shores of Nova Scotia as well.

In 1866, postmaster Wesley Crooks (who would one day be Canada's oldest living postmaster) must have believed the news arriving at his post office that the Fenians were attacking villages along the shores of Nova Scotia. When it was reported that the Fenians were pillaging nearby French Village, he mustered men, guns and ammunition and marched inland to ward off the attackers. Alas, there was no raid and the men endured hard weather and a difficult foray, only to return home exhausted.

5

The Keeper of the Light

Peggy's Cove today with reminders of the past.

The first lighthouse at Peggy's Cove, built in 1868, was a rather modest wooden structure of about eight square metres with a large lantern for a light on the roof. The lamp was fuelled by kerosene and magnified by a silver-coated mirror known as a catoptric reflector, creating a reddish glow that could be seen at sea. It was lit each evening by Edward Horn, who had the honour of being the Cove's first lightkeeper. Mr. Horn, who lived in the lighthouse, was paid $350 per year for keeping the light and attempting to warn hapless captains at sea of the dangers of the rocks. In 1872, some improvements in the way of a finished storeroom and two bedrooms made the lighthouse more serviceable and livable.

One can only imagine the difficulties Edward Horn confronted as he attempted to ensure that the light remained visible through the night during some of those raging winter storms when visibility would be close to zero and any ship tossing about in the sea would not know its fate probably until it was far too late to change course and head back to the deep for relative safety.

A southeast gale on April 15, 1881, walloped the Cove and damaged the foundation of the lighthouse considerably.

Waves must have washed right through the first floor since the lighthouse's heat supply, an oil stove, and much of the interior contents were swept away. As someone who has more than once had to move an old Nova Scotian oil stove, I can attest that such a beast is a heavy, obstinate object requiring massive effort to budge. The waves that roared through the lighthouse that April must have been formidable. After the storm, the lighthouse was repaired and the stove replaced at the cost of $545.

Although I could find no newspaper accounts, local lore suggests that there was a major shipwreck in the area in the 1880s. An American schooner foundered on the rocks in yet another fierce storm. There is no mention of survivors but the bodies of three sailors washed in and were found in one of the several low-lying saltwater ponds along the coast. The sailors were respectfully buried nearby and the pond is now known as Sailor's Pond.

Another storm in 1898 dislodged a 66-ton boulder and deposited it in front of the lighthouse, where it remains today, a forbidding reminder of the occasional ferocity of nature. It was also that same storm that floated the general store and moved it from its resting place to the water's edge, where it was halved and propped on stilts to become the gathering place known as "Parliament House."

A fire swept through the small St. John's Chapel in 1884 and burned it to the ground and, on April 26 of the next year, the larger St. John's Anglican Church was built with its gothic spire that can be seen from the surrounding countryside. This is the church that is still standing today. Visitors can enter the church during posted times throughout the summer.

St. John's Church, 1944.

In 1956, artist and sculptor, William E. deGarthe would describe the church in glowing terms:

> A more fitting architectural design could not have been chosen to blend so perfectly in with its surroundings, greeting the visitors from near and far, with its red roof and the tall slender spire, reaching to the sky, white-painted sides and gothic windows, empha-sizing the height by its lathed walls. It is a very beautiful artistic structure, and a tribute to its unknown designer.

Helen Creighton (1899-1989) was Nova Scotia's pre-eminent folklorist who travelled the province with notebook and tape recorder, gathering stories of local belief, customs, songs and recollections of older residents, especially those

St. John's Anglican Church today.

in coastal communities. Peggy's Cove was a rich source of material dating back into the nineteenth century and in her book *Bluenose Magic*, she records some of what she found there.

Creighton discovered a wealth of superstitions still alive or at least remembered. White mittens, for example, were the only ones to be worn aboard ship. Bad luck came with wearing even grey mittens. Nails were never to be hammered into the mainmast. (This may have its logical applications, of course, as a nail through a mast could set in motion a fracture that may one day bring that mast down in a strong gale.) To see a crow flying over the bow would be considered bad luck. It was also said that someone born with a caul, a filmy membrane over the head left over from the birth, was protected from drowning. This was an old English belief noted in literature as far back as 1547 that undoubtedly found its way to the small outport. Captains around the Cove would be more than pleased to take on a local man known to be born with a caul if only to help ensure the safety of their ships.

Helen Creighton found no evidence of witches being drowned, hanged or burned in Nova Scotia but she did find stories that suggested belief in witchcraft was widespread, especially in Peggy's Cove. People spoke of "bewitched" cattle and "cursed" individuals in the eighteenth, nineteenth and into the twentieth century. A broom across the door would keep out witches since they could not step over broom handles.

As recently as 1904, a girl nearby in St. Margaret's Bay was supposedly accosted by a woman accused of being a witch. The girl's father brought in a Lunenburg "witch doctor" by the name of Joe Weeno (possibly Veinotte), who showed up as a kind of witch hit man. The witch doctor killed a pig, planted nine carved knives of wood into the pig's warm heart and threw the heart into the fire. The ashes from the fire were then used to mark the door of the supposed victim's house with a cross to keep the witch away. As the story is told, the witch either died (possibly at the hands of the father) or simply never was seen again.

With medical help at considerable distance, folk cures and remedies would sometimes have to suffice. It was believed the seventh son of a seventh son could perform many amazing feats, including curing someone of a rash known as the "king's evil." And if lying in a feather bed sometimes caused rheumatism as superstition suggested, it could be cured by wearing a potato hung around your neck. As the potato dried out, the rheumatism would disappear. Nutmegs around the neck would work for getting rid of boils.

Should you be unlucky enough to jab a rusty nail in your hand, you were advised to put the nail in a barrel of cod oil and that would cure the infection. If you tripped over some fishing gear on the dock and thought you might have busted a rib, put some grains of barley in a glass. If they float, then you have a broken rib. If not, you're just a little sore and things will feel better in a day or two … as long as the air pressure doesn't drop too dramatically.

No Fisherman's Friend lozenges were available in the single local store in the 1800s, but should you come down with a sore throat, a pair of split salt herring put into a rag and held to the neck should have you feeling better sooner or later, although it would not do much for your love life.

Warts could be cured by stealing a piece of pork. (I'm not sure why it had to be stolen but that was part of the deal.) The stolen pork was rubbed over the wart and then buried.

Creighton also came across the story of a woman named Mary Ann visiting the Cove in the late 1800s. She cured a boy with severe nosebleeds by providing the lad with a fragment of paper with some words written on it. The boy was to carry the paper in his pocket and the nose bleeding would stop. Sure enough, this did the trick, although the storyteller did not know what the secret words were and so this cure is lost forever to modern medicine.

Since hard science and meteorology were not readily available to the people of a small coastal community, there were a considerable number of superstitions that prevailed to predict events and weather. A tea leaf floating on the top of a cup meant a visitor was coming. To discover the day of arrival, the leaf was put on the back of the left hand made into a fist and the days of the week would be announced. The arrival would coincide to the naming of the day when the leaf would stick to the skin.

If you were a fisherman, taking your life in your hands each and every time you went to sea, predicting bad weather was a serious business. Much of it was common sense, although it was often mixed with superstition. Gulls flying high and circling in packs predicted high winds were coming. This occurrence is not as common as it sounds unless you are at Peggy's Cove on any given high-density tourist day when the gulls are watching the unwary visitors, waiting for them to leave a bag of chips unattended or drop parts of a sandwich on the rocks.

Gulls do circle before a serious storm. According to superstition, a full moon also means high winds. But then if you live by the coast, you are bound to have strong winds as a common phenomenon so almost anything could be seen as a "prediction." Certainly some people can sense the air pressure dropping and, if you lived near the coast, you'd turn to them for advice as to whether the morrow be calm or stormy.

In *Richard Zurawski's Book of Maritime Weather*, the author documents some of the other common folk methods for predicting weather. You could watch animals – cows and dogs in particular – and they would give clues as to storms coming in. Dogs with more acute hearing may also hear thunder farther off and give an indication with their attentiveness that a storm was arriving. Most birds react to the air pressure, geese and ducks in particular. High-flying geese mean high pressure and good weather. Low-flying geese suggest low pressure and bad weather. Bees, they say, also tend to stay closer to hives if bad weather is coming.

"Red sky at night, sailors' delight. Red sky at morning, sailors take warning," is the old adage that just happens to be true most of the time. It was said that if you had "March in January," you'd end up with "January in March" and he "who doffs his coat on a winter's day will gladly put it on in May."

Another old coastal saying goes:

> A veering wind, fair weather
> A backing wind, foul weather
> If the wind back against the sun
> Trust it not, for it will run.

Superstition or not, the people living in Peggy's Cove through the years understood the nature of wind, and even a child would quickly learn to notice which direction the wind came from. Fishermen would discuss the weather endlessly with great passion and sometimes disdain. There were surprises, of course, and they could sometimes be deadly. But to anyone living in the Cove, an understanding of the weather was essential.

6

"A Small Basin in the Mighty Rock"

A quiet morning in the Cove.

At the turn of the twentieth century, Peggy's Cove was an active, mostly self-contained little fishing community. The lives of the families, as always, were tied to the sea. In the higher tides of October and November, boats were hauled ashore and, through the winter months, the nets were repaired. Only the brave, desperate or foolhardy would go to sea in the stormy winter months when the air temperature went down to -20° Celsius and the sea temperature hovered near freezing. In the spring, the boats would be scraped and fresh copper-based paints applied to prevent barnacle and moss growth and rot. As the days warmed and the seas subsided, the fishing boats slipped back into the cool dark waters of the sea where fishermen continued the trade of their fathers and grandfathers.

Eels were captured in lakes and streams nearby, in baskets made from handwoven saplings, and some freshwater fish were caught as well – often by the young boys in the community, those too young to go to sea with their fathers.

Around 1900 the owners of nearby lobster processing factories sent their own boats, called "smacks," around to the smaller villages to collect the catch that they would process. Fishermen were now paid $1.50 per hundred lobsters.

This modern gourmet seafood was then still very much considered to be a lower-class dish. Lobster sandwiches would have been a staple for many coastal families when it was in season. It was not too long, however, before lobster fishing would go into one of several serious declines that would see the closing of the plants and the loss of income for families in the Cove.

The mouth of Peggy's Cove had always been peppered with many large boulders sticking up out of the water or lurking just below the waves. Generations of fathers had taught their sons how to navigate the tricky entrance to the little harbour. In 1900, at long last, many of these large rocks were cleared away so larger vessels could enter and buy the fish caught by local fishermen.

The removal of the rocks proved to be high entertainment for everyone in town as the process was quite elaborate. Two large vessels anchored in the appropriate location and planks were laid down between them to provide a working surface. Long hand drills and hard labour were involved in drilling holes into the offending granite. Sticks of dynamite were dropped into place and villagers were thrilled by the spectacle of massive boulders being blown apart. At low tide, workmen wrapped chains around some of the larger pieces left over and, when the tide rose again to allow for boats to pass, the larger pieces were towed out to deeper waters for deposit.

It was also in 1900 that the Orange Lodge was built, suggesting something of the political flavour of the community. The Orange Order was a Protestant "fraternal" organization founded in Ireland in 1795 that celebrated the victory of William of Orange at the 1790 Battle of the

The entrance to Peggy's Cove today.

Boyne. The organization, which kept alive Protestant Irish folklore and politics, had its own set of rituals like the Masons and there was a strong undercurrent of anti-Catholic sentiment in some sectors. In nineteenth-century Canada, the Orangemen had played a key role in the formation of national politics after Confederation. The Orange Order, however, also helped to weld together like-minded people in isolated communities like Peggy's Cove and the new lodge became an important centre of social activities. The hall was later rebuilt and enlarged in the 1950s and used for dances and church socials.

While Peggy's Cove was certainly not the tourist destination it is today, travel writers following in the footsteps of

Joseph Howe felt compelled to visit the quaint village and write eloquent impressions of the stark beauty of the place and of its people. One such anonymous journalist, writing for the *Novascotian*, trekked there in 1903 and called it, "The roughest, rockiest and wildest point on the iron bound coast of Nova Scotia." The population seems to have been on the decline from 400 as the writer notes that, at one time, the Cove had upwards of 300 school children but by 1903 there were only seventeen children and no teacher. Many young men had gone to sea in bigger ships perhaps out of Halifax or Lunenburg, and certain numbers of young men and women alike had been lured to a better life in the "Boston States" – Boston or other New England towns and cities. Some families had decided life was more comfortable inland as the ups and downs of fish prices had made for an uncertain life once a family was tied into a cash economy rather than simply working for their own subsistence.

The *Novascotian* travel writer seemed dismissive of the beauties of the place, noting that it had no beaches or protection from the foamy bashing waves as did Chester farther along St. Margaret's Bay. Chester, the author noted with pride, was already a favoured resort for wealthy Americans. The writer went on to say, "Peggy's Cove is nothing but a small basin in the mighty rock on which the village is built, but it affords shelter for half a hundred fishing boats and is the reason why the United Empire Loyalists, who, refusing to give up their allegiance to King George, decided to make their homes here."

There's an odd mix of arrogance and possibly misguided politics in that statement that might be hard to fathom today. Any thoughts of King George III and Crown loyalty would surely have long faded by 1903 in the Cove. My guess is that folks were more concerned with the day-to-day realities of fish stocks, fish prices and whether they had enough sustenance to get the family through a hard winter. Nor did the visiting journalist seem to appreciate the safer entrance to the harbour thanks to the ambitious blasting of boulders.

The journalist admitted that the Cove had a few attractions. There was the Coffin Rock with a hole said to be the exact shape and size of a casket. Someone reported that it had been carved out by the mutinous crew of an American brig who had murdered their captain and buried the body in a boulder. It was a good story, but I doubt the Halifax writer (who would clearly rather have been assigned a more civilized locale like Chester or Mahone Bay) was willing to buy into the idea that mutineers would have bothered to spend days, if not weeks, chiselling solid granite to bury the evidence of their foul deed.

And the reporter was also introduced to the Devil's Armchair, a rock shaped like a chair, where it was said Satan sat on the stormiest of nights. Now that seems somewhat more likely true to anyone who has had the chance to observe the fiercest of the nor'easters that sweep by the shores here and pound the bald rocks with such ferocity that it stuns the senses.

In the Cove, the *Novascotian* reported, only one man was not a Tory, that is to say a member of the day's Conservative party, and everyone was an Episcopalian, this at least partially owing to the fact that this was the only church for miles around. The visiting journalist was satisfied that "the community was at peace with itself," or at least so it seemed to a roving reporter anxious to leave the wild barren world of Peggy's Cove and return to the urban comforts of Halifax. One could assume, however, that the community was not rife with major family squabbles or religious bickering. But the sad truth was that the fishing was not good. Even the rector of the church, presumably the Reverend John Arnold, who served from 1899 to 1909, grieved in his sermon about the bad times and prayed with his congregation for a return to the days of abundant fish. "Unless the fish come back again," the writer reported, "a very few years will see the place deserted."

There was little in the way of alternate employment in the community except for the postmaster job and that of the lightkeeper. Edward Horn had turned the lightkeeping over to W. Crooks in 1874 and he in turn passed the job on to S.J. Massie in 1878. Next in line were lightkeepers G. Swinnehammer (1882-1902), and S.H. Garrison (1902-1926).

In 1914, the building of a new, substantially taller lighthouse at Peggy's Point began on the solid granite rock about fifty-four feet from the original wooden structure. The cost would amount to $2,457 for the sixty-seven-foot tall building. The lantern and its installation cost nearly as much. On August 1, 1915, the first beam from the new light spread out across the Atlantic from this formidable structure that would survive into the next century to be photographed by millions of tourists who would visit Peggy's Cove from around the world. The colour of the new light was white rather than red and penetrated thirteen miles into the night, thanks to the use of a more sophisticated dioptric lens involving a set of glass prisms.

This new lens, developed by French physicist Augustin Jean Fresnel, had proven to be a revolutionary improvement for lighthouses around the world.

1915 was a year of other improvements as well, with two new breakwaters constructed to make the harbour safer for all concerned. One was built at the mouth of the Cove to decrease the danger of ships being swamped when storm waves surged around the point. The second was built at the rear of the Cove on a marshland, presumably to avoid flooding at the higher tides of the year.

7

Rum on the Rocks

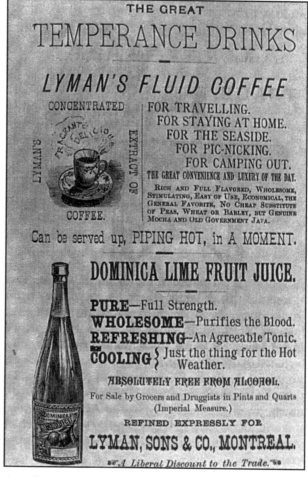

An advertisement for non-alcoholic temperance drinks.

The story of booze, legal and illegal, is inextricably woven into the history of the province of Nova Scotia. The French and English military brought great stores of wine, brandy, ale and gin across the Atlantic for their soldiers and sailors. Rum found its way in vast quantities to these shores during the golden era of sailing ships when Bluenose captains sailed south to trade with the islands of the Caribbean and returned home with dark, plentiful, inexpensive rum made from sugar cane.

Halifax in the nineteenth century had a reputation for being the roughest booze-sodden seaport on the east coast of North America, and there was a spillover of drink and its various problems into the rest of the province. If West Indies rum was not readily available, then there was moonshine to be made from distilled molasses.

From early on there was a backlash from the church and from organizations such as Nova Scotia's Sons of Temperance, "The Oldest Total Abstinence Organization in North America." Even before the temperance movement blossomed, wives had been looking for ways to cure their husbands of their fondness for drink. Helen Creighton reported the following folk method to make a man go sober: "To cure a man of drink, take an eel and put [it] in rum, but don't leave the eel in long enough to die. Then give the rum to the person to drink, but don't tell him about the eel. If he drinks it he will never touch rum again." Certainly the eels were readily available, caught in the handwoven baskets in the ponds near Peggy's Cove. But whether the cure worked or not is unknown. It is probable, though, that drunkenness was not quite as prevalent in the tight-knit Episcopalian community as it was in the urban squalor of Halifax.

Instead, Peggy's Cove and its relation to alcohol didn't become significant until well into the 1920s when the American Volstead Act created Prohibition and rum-running became a way of life for many fishermen who were floundering on hard times. The 1920s was a time of economic depression and it had a devastating impact on the folks of rural Nova Scotia who were already quite poor. To add insult to injury, the United States had banned Canadian fisherman from landing their catch freely at American ports – a long-standing tradition. Duty was added to any fish products coming from Canada. The fishery plummeted even deeper into ruin and, while it was still possible to catch fish for your own family to eat, earning a wage to buy other basic necessities had become exceedingly difficult.

So it is little wonder that many fishermen along the South Shore turned to smuggling rum and other forms of alcohol into the United States. By January 1925, the *Maritime Merchant* reported that somewhere between fifty and a hundred Lunenburg fishing vessels were involved in smuggling. And there were many more than that coming from the smaller ports like Peggy's Cove, Indian Harbour and West Dover. According to rum historian Ernest Forbes, there were many women, especially single mothers who had no access to any form of welfare, who became involved in one way or the other in the illegal but potentially lucrative business.

Off the coast of Peggy's Cove and at numerous locations along the South Shore, fishermen who had converted their boats into rum-runners would meet up with larger ships, many from the French islands of St. Pierre and Miquelon, and take on as much liquor as they could carry. The trick then was to move it into American waters and ashore to a willing buyer without getting caught. By 1924, the U.S. had converted naval destroyers and smaller craft to chase and apprehend rum-runners. They succeeded often, but there were far too many rum-runners to catch them all.

Farther south, the patrols were heavier. The U.S. had no jurisdiction outside its twelve-mile limit, but along the South Shore of Nova Scotia, the American customs agents had no jurisdiction at all so it was relatively safer to make contact with a foreign ship and offload as many crates of hard liquor as your vessel could carry. (Sometimes the wood left over from the crates was used to make wooden shingles for barns and sheds.) After that it was often a matter of hiding out in one of the many coves or inlets, or, for the daring, even tying up for the night at the wharf in Peggy's Cove and waiting for the best weather conditions to make a run for the coast of New England to supply the ever-anxious buyers there.

In order to avoid capture, rum-runners would take unusual, sometimes more dangerous passages or create smokescreens using oil and rags on the exhaust to provide a cover for themselves.

Some residents around St. Margaret's Bay were prosecuted for their involvement in the smuggling. Nearby Tantallon was a centre of serious rum-running where occasionally the liquor was stored ashore. Locals opposed to alcohol consumption, it is said, were loathe to turn in their neighbour to the police but on occasion would foul the booze by adding kerosene or some other ungodly flavouring to make it undrinkable. After Prohibition, people found kegs of rum buried in piles of sawdust and in the backyards once owned by rum-runners.

Some rum-runners made fortunes. Stories of the criminal adventure are abundant. Some of the rum-runners, fearful of the law, kept tight lips. Others, once Prohibition was lifted, spoke freely if not always truthfully about their escapades. In many respects, rum-running has been glorified in the history of this province. That's just the kind of people we are.

According to J.F.B. Livesay in his 1944 book, *Peggy's Cove,* a Canadian government vessel tried to catch a rum-runner from Indian Harbour during the height of Prohibition. The rum-runner had reportedly made contact with the mother ship, taken on the goods and was making for home port when the authorities gave chase. As he rounded the point at Peggy's Cove, the smuggler shut off his engines and slipped into the narrow opening of the harbour, eluding the pursuer's boat and tying up for the night. When the government boat showed up the next morning, the runner was tied up at Rupert's stage. The captain of the government ship was said to be "hopping mad" as there was not a pint of rum to be found aboard. And it's safe to say it wasn't consumed all in one night at Peggy's Cove, although it's likely that a few glasses were raised to the success of the venture.

Robert R. Manuel was hired in 1934 to tend to the lighthouse. According to Harry Thurston, the Cove must have already garnered considerable notoriety because Manuel said he had acted as tour guide, taking as many as 1,800 people up to see the lamp at the top of the lighthouse. Manuel eventually quit the practice, claiming it took too much time away from the important job of keeping the light functioning as it should.

Bob Davis, writing in the Halifax *Evening Mail* on August 30, 1934, reported that the community of Peggy's Cove had only one radio and one telephone. He seemed surprised that there was no jail or any form of medical service available. The nearest doctor was in Seabright ten miles away. In many respects, the village was still a fairly self-sufficient community.

Peggy's Cove did have a postmaster, however. Wesley Crooks would keep the job until he was well into his nineties, setting a record as the oldest postmaster in Canada. His record claim to fame still stands today. Wesley would be the source of much of the history and lore of the Cove that he passed on to William deGarthe for his book, *This is Peggy's Cove, Nova Scotia*. It was in 1934 that Crooks decided he'd licked enough stamps for one man and he retired, turning the postal business over to his son, L.A. Crooks.

Douglas Pope, in his biography of deGarthe, describes the post office of that day. The Crooks home was a small, two-storey dwelling with a good view of the lighthouse. When the mail arrived, it was piled on the kitchen table

The large boulder by the road leading to the Cove.

next to the woodstove. Neighbours, who entered from the back door, often showed up before it was sorted and watched or helped to see who had anything interesting to pick up that day. Tourists, however, usually came in the front door and were served in the somewhat more formal setting of Crooks' living room.

The mail business remained in the family for a good long time. It was handed over to Gertie Crooks, who ran the post office from her home up until 1969, at which time it was moved into the only restaurant in Peggy's Cove.

I'm sure no one who lived in the Cove during the first half of the twentieth century could ever have envisioned it becoming the tourist mecca it is today, attracting cruise ship visitors, Harley-Davidson bikers and people from the four corners of the earth. When the American writer T. Morris Longstreth arrived in the Thirties, he would have found it quaint that there was still a gate at the entrance to Peggy's

Peggy's Cove – Lesley Choyce

Cove. The gate, located by that giant boulder that still sits by the road as you enter the village, had remained there for a long time, supposedly to keep cows from straying into the backyards and gardens. Young, hopeful entrepreneurs would hang around the gate in the summers and wait for visitors. They'd open the gate for them and hope for a tip of five or ten cents from the more generous visitors on an excursion to the lighthouse and rocks.

Longstreth, a very well-known travel writer of his day, did predict that tourists would one day "discover" Peggy's Cove and the people and the village would lose its "character." Alas, he sighed, it would become a tourist trap. Later, however, in a 1947 *Maclean's Magazine* article called "Seaside Shangri-La," Ian Sclanders disagreed with the American writer, stating, "Longstreth underestimated them [the people of Peggy's Cove]. He didn't realize that they have absorbed some of the changelessness of their native rocks."

8

A Wharf, a War and an Army of Artists

Captain Alton with Clyde and Albert Crooks.

Some disasters at sea forever remain a mystery. Once a ship is lost, those ashore can only attempt to fit together the pieces of whatever evidence remains and try to imagine the details of the tragedy, even as they mourn for those lost to the depths of the sea. Such is the case of the *Clarisse*, reported by Robert C. Parsons in his book *The Edge of Yesterday: Sea Disasters of Nova Scotia*. The *Clarisse* had been a leaky ship in for repairs in North Sydney, Cape Breton, in the late summer of 1938. The fifty-five-ton "coaster" had taken on coal in Cape Breton and was headed to Tancook Island. Captain Joseph Fyfe, famous in Sydney for having helped to forge the first all-Canadian route to the gold rush in the Yukon, was captain, assisted by his son, Aubrey.

The buildup of coal gases or some other cause led to an explosion on the *Clarisse* on September 7 or 8 off the shores of Peggy's Cove and all were lost at sea. The RCMP cutter *Fleur de Lis* searched the area and found debris but no bodies. A week later, two men from nearby West Dover – Sandford and Freeman Morash – found a washed up coal scoop, a foghorn and some ship planks, all believed to have been from the *Clarisse*. But like so many other catastrophes in the North Atlantic, the true cause of the accident would never be known.

Despite the all too common bad news of disaster at sea, there must have been some celebrating among area residents in 1938 when the St. Margaret's Bay Road was paved for the first time. It was still a pretty bumpy ride, however, for anyone brave enough to take on the potholes, protruding rocks and frost heaves of any of the secondary roads that snaked through Shad Bay, West Dover, Peggy's Cove and Indian Harbour. And life itself in the Cove had not become any easier.

Farming anywhere around the village had never been easy. The soil was thin and the bedrock exposed in many places. Kitchen gardens produced cabbages, turnips, potatoes and a few greens but there was little in the way of fertile acreage for significant crops. There were chickens caged and a few running around the village. Hogs had been raised by a few but the relatively close quarters of the Cove did not make them popular. A small herd of dairy cows grazed beyond the houses on the meadows and there were four or five oxen used mostly for haying. Wesley Crooks had bought a horse to do his hay harvesting, but most agreed that an ox was better adapted to work on the rugged land where rocks were plentiful.

The price of fish was now so low that most fishermen felt it wasn't worth their while to fish for commercial purposes. They'd fish to feed their families and to heck with bothering to sell their catch to the buyers who themselves were not in a position to offer an honest price for the hard labour of hauling in the catch. Thus fishermen around the

Cutting and hauling hay near the Cove.

harbour could be seen mending nets, scraping and painting their boats, reminiscing about the departed good old times that seemed gone forever. Some went inland for work in the woods or took up other trades. Travel author J.F.B. Livesay recounts of this slow time, "And so it was the women who did the work, laundry-day every working day, the Cove aflutter with billowing linen." So at least everyone had clean sheets to sleep on through the long cold nights. Not only were the sheets clean, but so was the pristine water of the Cove according to Livesay, who also noted that only on rare occasions did the water get so choked with cut-off cod heads with their vacant staring eyes that they needed to be "dredged" out to deeper water. Obviously, there were still plenty of fish to be caught and cleaned; it was just a very poor market for selling fish.

A few of the fishermen with the proper gear found a market for tuna, or "albacore" as it was referred to then.

The going price was twenty cents a pound, drastically less than the small fortune that Nova Scotia tuna is worth today on the Japanese fish trading markets. Tuna ranged in weight from fifty to 800 pounds, however, so if you caught a really big fish, you could earn $160, which would have more than pleased a wife who spent her days washing your laundry. But such instances were rare. Tuna had been fished off these shores by local and foreign ships for two centuries. In the Cove, it had been part of the diet – but often considered to be difficult, dangerous work. Cod or haddock was preferred and was certainly an easier catch. Over the years, tuna had also been prized for its oil, which was used in the tanning of leather. On into the future, tuna from off the coast of Peggy's Cove would find its way into those world markets where it was esteemed for its use in sushi and other Japanese delicacies.

If the sea could not always provide an income, it never failed to offer up surprises. On February 4, 1940, Richard Crooks saw something thrashing around beneath his own wharf. It turned out to be a "horned sea monster," and for whatever reasons, a few of the locals took it upon themselves to kill it with axes, which must have been a strange and horrifying site for any children or women who happened to be in attendance. No one had ever seen such a thing before. It had two small horns on its head, eyes like a pig, a hinged *upper* jaw, three small fins and a tail like a porpoise. The beast was fourteen feet long and weighed roughly a ton.

Seabright resident Lester Hubley bought the dead sea monster – hoping probably to profit in some way by exhib-

Reuben Crooks mending a net.

iting the hapless creature. It took twenty-three men with a block and tackle to load the great sea creature into Lester's truck, and it must have been quite a sight to see Hubley driving his sea monster – and what he hoped to be the source of instant wealth – through the small communities on his way to Halifax. Hubley transported the poor dead beast to government fisheries expert R. A. MacKenzie, who wasn't quite as impressed as Hubley thought he should be. MacKenzie simply reported that it was some sort of strange whale and probably not worthy of anyone's price of admission to a fish freak show.

Certainly the creature would have been of greater interest alive but no one was about to cart a living sea monster around the province in the bed of a truck. And, undoubtedly, the kinder thing to do would have been to leave the beast alone, allowing the tide to rise and take the unique visitor back to the depths from which it had risen. But such was not the case. In the end, the headline in the Halifax paper read, "Experts Scratch Heads," and I'm sorry to report that I don't know what became of Hubley's odd critter after that.

One possible explanation is that the so-called "monster" was a coelacanth, a sea creature that was once believed to have gone extinct seventy million years ago. But then, one day in 1938, a coelacanth was caught off the coast of South Africa. On rare occasions, others had been caught or spotted, so there is some convincing evidence that this bizarre survivor of ancient times still haunts the depths and is responsible for many of the sea monster sightings down through the years. It is unlikely that the Peggy's Cove visitor of 1940 was a deformed whale and it may have been truly that rare anomaly, the coelacanth, although no one can say for sure. And there's always the possibility that another strange visitor like this might arrive here one day, hopefully to a friendlier greeting, and then the true identity might be determined.

The following year, government planners delivered a blueprint for a new wharf – a "government wharf," of which there would be many around the province. The men of the Cove were paid to build the wharf in the design and location proscribed by the so-called experts from away. It turned out that the location was a poor choice as it was too shallow for the bigger boats to come alongside.

In September of that year another fierce storm swamped the harbour, washing through and over the concrete dam at the harbour head. Some people were left "marooned," cut off from the mainland on the lighthouse rocks for awhile. Several wharves were hammered and fishing stages damaged. Although such storms wreaked havoc and threatened lives, no one was particularly surprised, and immediately afterward, repairs would begin. Wharves would be fortified and no families retreated inland to safer properties. The people here held a powerful sentimental attachment to the place and to their homes.

In 1940, the most recently built home in the Cove was fifty years old and Ian Sclanders would write a few years later that the houses seemed architecturally reminiscent of wooden ships – in their construction perhaps, but not in their looks. He noted that they were brightly painted, making for a tidy, clean-looking village.

The famous lighthouse that loomed over the Cove was improved several times in the 1940s. The old oil lamp and petroleum vapour flame was replaced by a "duplex-flat wick lamp." An electric beacon was tried for awhile but then the lightkeeper returned to using oil. In 1949, however, the light source was shifted once again to electricity and thus it has remained an electric light to this day, upgraded several times to increase its candlepower.

During World War II, the Royal Canadian Navy conducted what it called "shake up" manoeuvers in St. Margaret's Bay. Peggy's Cove lighthouse was put to use as a radio station. There had been numerous sightings of German submarines as the enemy freely patrolled the Nova Scotia coastline. Spies were said to have come ashore from the subs, some of them living among South Shore residents of German descent. Exactly what they would discover of military importance concerning life around St. Margaret's Bay is difficult to say. Certainly, though, many of the reports of Nazi "spies" are credible. Germans had come ashore during the war years at many locations in Nova Scotia but it's easy to imagine how the stories were exaggerated through gossip-driven conversation concerning old German families, newcomers or strangers with unusual accents.

The danger of the German U-boats, however, were as real as it could get. Warships and civilian vessels had been targeted and crippled not far from the shores of the province throughout the war. The last Canadian military vessel to be sunk by U-boat attack was the HMCS *Esquimalt* on April 16, 1945, somewhat west of Peggy's Cove, not far from the approaches to Halifax Harbour. *U-190* had left Norway in February of that year with twenty-five-year-old Hans-Edwin Reith in command. He failed to sink two merchant vessels but then sighted the *Esquimalt*.

In command of the *Esquimalt* was Robert Macmillan (father of Nova Scotian musician Scott Macmillan), whose job it was to search and destroy enemy submarines in the approaches to the harbour, but his men and electronic gear failed to detect *U-190*. Reith realized his advantage, surfaced less than a half mile from the Canadian ship and fired a torpedo that ripped a great hole in the *Esquimalt*. The ship took on water and sank less than four minutes after the attack.

Many men were trapped in the sinking ship but those who could get overboard helped each other into the emergency rafts. Sadly, a plane flew over and had spotted the rafts but the pilot thought them to be fishing boats. Two minesweepers were in the vicinity, but their captains also failed to realize the emergency nearby as news had not reached command headquarters of the hit. Six men paddled towards the *Halifax East Light Vessel* and were rescued. The minesweeper *Sarnia* pulled twenty-one others aboard six hours after the *Esquimalt* went down. All the men were cold and suffering. Forty-four died in the disaster.

Reith had taken the *U-190* into shallow waters to avoid his pursuing adversaries and his U-boat was not detected. He headed for Germany but later received news of Germany's surrender and he, himself, surrendered his submarine and crew in St. John's, Newfoundland on May 11, 1945.

Peggy's Cove certainly never sustained any wartime attack. However, after the war, the one-and-a-half storey lightkeeper's home was abandoned and the Department of National Defence deemed it unfit for human inhabitation. Later DND would offer it for sale to anyone who wanted to lug the building away. Sadly, there were no takers and, on March 17, 1955, it was demolished and the rubble was hauled away.

Mora Dianne O'Neill, in her book *Paintings of Nova Scotia: From the Collection of the Art Gallery of Nova Scotia*, notes that Ottawa sent Marius Barbeau from the National Museum to Halifax in 1933 to chastise the art community of the province. He told an audience at the Canadian Club of Halifax that "Nova Scotia lags behind the rest of Canada in art." There was a snobbish tone to his speech that did not sit well with Haligonians who rather liked the plethora of paintings produced of quaint South Shore coastal villages of which Peggy's Cove was the crown jewel. One local reviewer complained, however, that at provincial art shows, "eighty-eight percent of the entries ... are devoted to fishing villages and rocks," but that did not deter painters from making pilgrimages to Peggy's Cove with palette, brush and canvas.

After the war, some in government and commerce were beginning to see tourism as a bright opportunity on the horizon for Nova Scotia. It was clear that artists painting Peggy's Cove and displaying the paintings nationally or internationally could spark more interest in people coming here on vacation and spending their money. There was also a provincial program, Nova Scotia Pictures, begun in 1946, that toured art exhibitions around the province. By 1950, 150,000 people had viewed 362 Nova Scotia paintings, many of them of rocks and fishing shacks with a more than generous representation of life in Peggy's Cove. Well-known artists from outside the province, such as Kathleen Daly

Pepper and George Pepper, were also using the Cove as a subject for their work. Although no one could possibly document the total number of Peggy's Cove paintings created by the armies of artists who have descended on the village over the years, it's safe to say that the number would be in the thousands. And of photographs taken of the Cove, professional and amateur, it would be in the millions.

9

"A Main Street Paved with Saltwater"

Children of the Cove, circa 1944.

Ian Sclanders, in his 1947 *Maclean's Magazine* article, brought national attention to Peggy's Cove with a somewhat romanticized notion of life there. He referred to the harbour as "a Main Street paved with saltwater – because the commerce of the village revolves around its wharves and fish sheds." Sclanders provides some astute everyday details of a life far away from urban Toronto where readers would be charmed by the idyll of a coastal life.

There were only eleven wells in Peggy's Cove since they were so difficult to drill in the hard, unyielding rock, so some families shared. Because of those same rocks, the deceased had be buried six miles down the road in Hackett's Cove, where there was enough depth to the topsoil to make decent burial possible. Gardens, as previously noted, were difficult at best but Louis Crooks, the seventy-year-old postmaster (son of Wesley Crooks), did not let that deter him. With his boat and oxcart, he hauled enough soil to fill a large depression in the granite on his property and, with the help of a healthy dose of eelgrass, grew a good crop of fresh vegetables that he sold from his ever-popular post office. Where there's a will, there's clearly a way.

Sclanders counted seventy-five residents in all with only

nine students at the little school, ranging in ages from six to sixteen. If anyone became seriously ill, the doctor was fifteen miles away but there were black and white movies each Thursday at the community hall and a dance on Saturday night.

Household goods like cooking utensils and furniture had mostly been handed down within the family and the women still used scrub boards and tubs for washing clothes, while the woodstoves kept the houses warm and copper kettles atop those stoves boiled water for the tea. The white pine floors from generations past were kept clean with yellow soap and a hard-bristled brush.

Despite the seemingly primitive nature of home life here, Sclanders discovered plenty of good omens. There was no such thing as divorce, he claimed, and he was convinced by all he spoke to that crime simply did not exist. If problems came up in the community, a meeting was held at the local hall to talk it through. Wesley Crooks told him that "No man holds office" and every man owned his own home. There was some official mode of representation, however, in the form of a county councillor who did not live in the Cove but a fair distance inland in Glen Margaret.

Carloads of sightseers had begun to arrive, mostly in the summers. Sclanders reckoned that eighty to a hundred cars came to see the rocks, the lighthouse and the tiny houses surrounding the harbour in the warmer months. The local kids were still in charge of opening the famous village gate and were on hand to welcome travellers and receive a small tip of five to fifteen cents, depending on the largesse of the driver.

In the summer, a famous preacher, Reverend Dr. Robert Norwood, originally from Nova Scotia but now the minister at St. Bartholomew's Episcopal Church on Park Avenue, New York City, came to Peggy's Cove to preach at St. John's Church. Acclaimed as a great orator and poet, he packed the church to overflowing and delivered passionate resounding sermons to those assembled.

Promotion of Peggy's Cove by the province had begun to attract more and more artists, some of them fisherman wannabes that Sclanders said dressed "more like fishermen than the fishermen themselves, the standard uniform being blue cotton pants, flannel shirts and blue ring-necked sweaters."

Frank A. Doane, in his 1949 volume, *Nova Scotia Sketches*, referred to Peggy's Cove as a "Wonderland." Doane wrote of the Cove, "It holds visitors spellbound in wonder and amazement." Government recognition of the economic possibilities of exploiting tourism had brought out the road graders as well. "The newly graded and gravelled highway is appreciated by all travellers," Doane noted. "The prospect of having the road paved in the not too distant future assures a great increase in the number of tourists that then will visit the widely known and unique settlement." In other words, Peggy's Cove was now open to the world.

Doane himself was enchanted by the rocks. "How came this great mass of solid rock to be exposed on so large a scale in this place?" he asked. "Surely there is nothing like it elsewhere in the country." He suggests that the sheep trying to graze in such a place might need to "have their noses sharpened so that they could feed between the closely packed stones and rocks." Those large loose stones that sit upon the bare bedrock, he refers to as "ballast from Noah's Ark."

Doane inaccurately reports that there are no gardens, no grass, no fences, no goats, no hay, no cows and nor are there any wells. The wells were not obvious perhaps and I guess that the cows and goats were a little further inland that day. Clearly, the man's fascination with the rocks obscured his observation skills when it came to other more mundane things. He did, however, notice that "The women are good cooks," and "there are telephones, post office and regular bus service."

Doane was there in June when the lobster and cod fishing were over for the year but there was a "good run of mackerel" and the retail price for fresh fish was fifteen to twenty cents a piece, although most of it would be salted, packed in barrels and sent overseas to foreign markets.

Despite the new gravel road and a few modern conveniences, Doane observes, "To dwellers in more favourable communities it would appear incredible that such a place as Peggy's Cove should ever have been selected for settlement." But Peggy's Cove was settled by a hardy breed and their descendants who stayed on in the Cove learned to adapt and survive.

Every author, it seems, who ventured to the Cove spoke in superlatives about what they found there. The American travel writer George Matthew Adams suggests that all his other travels to the world's wonders could not compare to a sunset at Peggy's Cove. "In my memory book of beauty spots," he wrote, "I place all that I was able to drink into my being and paint upon the canvas of my heart, of Peggy's

Cove." He too found a fondness for the rocks: "The rocks there are smooth, washed by centuries of sea waves, by some so mad that they have bitten into the face of the rock and given it a thousand dimples. And there are gorges and steps and great platforms, so smooth that you could happily sleep upon them in a blanket."

Few visitors left the Cove unmoved. Nova Scotian author Will R. Bird, in his 1956 classic, *Off-Trail in Nova Scotia*, wrote, "You can go a hundred times to Peggy's Cove and you will be thrilled anew each time you go, for the sheer rock ledges and great steps on grey granite, and the shore view, with fish houses on stilts, and boats in small havens, is just a bit more intensified, it seems, than elsewhere."

As more paintings and magazine photographs found their way far and beyond in the 1950s, more and more tourists arrived, including the first generations of tour buses. In the late 1950s Bernard Morash opened the "Tea Room," boasting all of five tables, to cater to the town's many guests. The name was later changed to the Sou'Wester Restaurant and sold to Jack Campbell in 1966.

The lighthouse that was now appearing on postcards and tourist brochures was kept running by Robert Manuel until 1958, at which time he gave up the post and was replaced by electric and mechanical equipment. The son of the former lightkeeper became a caretaker of the building in 1959, earning $100 per year, and he stayed on until 1966.

Along with the influx of tourists came the problem of inexperienced landlubbers exposed to the potential dangers of walking around the granite outcroppings so close to the pounding waves. On many days, the sea posed little threat at all as long as the city slickers had reasonable shoes and avoided walking on the dark and slippery patches of stone or testing their land legs too close to the edge of the sea.

But big storms often brought more sightseers to gawk at the massive waves and untamed fury of the sea. In October of 1962, Hurricane Daisy passed by the coast of Nova Scotia with enough fanfare to draw a crowd who trekked from the parking lot to the lighthouse to watch the waves crash and send great spumes of saltwater vaulting into the air. Local residents warned visitors of the dangers, but many ignored the admonition of those who understood the deadly potential of those very waves.

Herbert Ralph Swindell had driven his family out from Halifax to show them what hurricane waves looked like. They were standing a hundred feet from the lighthouse on the bare rocks when a giant twenty-five-foot wave pounded the shore and, in its retreat, pulled Swindell and his nine-year-old son Ernest and fourteen-year-old daughter Nancy into the maelstrom of the foamy seas beyond. Four young men tried bravely to rescue them and succeeded in bringing Nancy back to shore. But as Mrs. Swindell watched in horror, her husband and son were pulled away from shore in the churning waters and lost. The headline in the Halifax *Chronicle-Herald* the next day would read, "Father, Son Swept to Death While Watching Storm." Sadly, the Swindells would not be the last sightseers to lose their lives on the rocks of Peggy's Cove.

In the early 1960s, the provincial government was beginning to recognize the unique nature of this tiny coastal village and the Peggy's Cove Commission was established to set up special land-use regulations to protect what was there and avoid inappropriate development. A preservation area was also established to safeguard the glacial barrens around the Cove. Although not everyone was in favour of restricted land use and "public protection," it was a necessary step to preserve what was still a pristine and singular coastal wilderness as well as an historic and beautiful traditional fishing village.

10

"The Age-Old Rocks"

Faces etched in granite from the deGarthe monument.

William deGarthe was a sculptor and artist who lived in Peggy's Cove from the mid-1950s to his death in 1983. He was a colourful figure who "helped put Peggy's Cove on the map" and is remembered fondly by all who knew him. Born in Kaslo, Finland, in 1907, deGarthe immigrated to Canada and settled in Nova Scotia at the age of nineteen. He bought a cottage at Peggy's Cove in 1948, but lived in Timberlea and operated a commercial art shop in Halifax. He later moved to Peggy's Cove with his wife, Agnes, and it was there he would undertake his life's work in painting and sculpture. Together they opened an art studio and sold paintings to visitors – the prices varied but many were sold for a flat rate of $35.

At various points in his life, he had studied art and sculpture in Montreal and at Mount Allison University, the Art Students League in New York and in Carrara and Pietrasanta, Italy. There had been attempts at settling into other professions, but art was his passion and deGarthe was determined to make a living from his chosen career and to make a name for himself.

Douglas Pope, in his Lancelot Press book *deGarthe: His Life, Marine Art and Sculpture*, provides a portrait of a man who tried hard to fit in and shed the label of an outsider or come-from-away. He hosted successful parties and bought a sailing boat but seemed to have more ambition for his art and less time for the pleasures of sailing. He bought local fish, hung them out to dry on his clothesline and then salted them down for the winter as his fishermen neighbours instructed.

The artist became a promoter of the Cove as a tourist destination, which he believed was both good for the residents and good for his art. In 1956, deGarthe had self-published *This is Peggy's Cove, Nova Scotia*, a short book based on the research and interviews he conducted with the older folks nearby. Thousands of copies have been sold over the years and it can still be purchased in the gift shop of the Sou'Wester for $3.95. He was more than a little responsible for keeping alive one version concerning the origin of the name of the Cove – the story about the woman named Peggy who washes ashore after a shipwreck and makes the Cove her home. Douglas Pope notes that, like the legendary Peggy, deGarthe too was an outsider who found his way here, settled in and became accepted as part of the Peggy's Cove community.

In describing deGarthe's particular artistic style, Pope suggests that it is as if he has "crossed Michelangelo with L'il Abner – heroic but folksy." In fact, deGarthe did study marble sculpture in Italy at the same school where Michelangelo had worked 350 years earlier. Another more unlikely influence was Salvador Dali, the eccentric and brilliant Spanish surrealist. One of deGarthe's more outrageous and imaginative paintings was modelled after a Dali painting and showed an image of Christ hovering over Peggy's Cove.

The artist was known to "perform" for whoever was in attendance, both at home and on his travels to Florida and beyond. He would paint in public, tell stories both real and imaginary, and then sell the painting on the spot to a willing buyer at whatever price fit the artist's whimsy.

William deGarthe created sculptures in marble, alabaster, sandstone, cement and bronze. It would be the stone, especially chiselling the difficult Nova Scotian granite, that would be the hardest on the bones, joints and muscles of the man determined to leave a physical legacy of his art and an homage to the people of the Cove.

In the 1970s, deGarthe began chipping away at the thirty-metre long granite wall in his backyard, declaring that he was "just playing." It was to become a memorial to the "men of the sea and their families." Over a ten-year period leading up to his death, deGarthe worked faithfully at his sculpture along with some help from former student René Barrette and his next-door neighbour, Donald Crooks. The figures in the stoneface include St. Michael, the guardian angel of fishermen, along with local fishermen with their wives and children, deGarthe's pet seagull Joe, and Peggy herself as imagined by the stone sculptor. A few of the characters in the rock remain somewhat more bulky in appearance than intended, some say, because deGarthe did not have a chance to put the finishing touches on them. He died of cancer in 1983 and is buried in the monument itself.

Not long before his death, deGarthe offered twenty-five of his paintings as a donation to the Art Gallery of Nova Scotia but was turned down. (Douglas Pope estimates their value at $140,000.) The gallery did own two deGarthe

A detail of the stone angel from the monument.

paintings but the artist must certainly have felt the sting of the insult to his generous offer. The art gallery in Peggy's Cove featuring deGarthe's work was opened beside the monument in 1994 and is a popular stopoff point for tourists today.

In William deGarthe's poem, "Ode to Peggy's Cove," he writes,

> Man may change the Cove at will
> With dwellings, houses, stores – and still
> The age-old rocks ... of eons born
> Will stand, and man may pass, forever go ...

Fishing all along this coast continued to decline in the 1970s and that shifted employment away from the tradi-

deGarthe's memorial to the "men of the sea and their families."

tional livelihood. There was still some inshore fishing and prices remained high for tuna brought ashore and shipped to Japan. Lobster continued to be a valuable commodity but the legal season for trapping lobsters in local waters is from December to May, a difficult and dangerous time of year to be in the rough coastal waters dropping and retrieving the heavy, unwieldy lobster traps.

Although everyone knew it would be a good thing to maintain the look and feel of a traditional fishing village, it was becoming clear to everyone that the future of the Cove was in tourism and not fish. In 1978, Canada Post opened a seasonal post office for the tourists inside the lighthouse itself. It was such a hit with the visitors that it became a permanent fixture and now remains the only lighthouse post office in Canada. Every postcard or letter mailed there is stamped with a special cancellation mark in the shape of a lighthouse.

Federal and provincial funding helped bring about needed renovations to the Sou'Wester and its surroundings in 1988. Water had always been a problem for the restaurant and its thousands of visitors, so a large underground water tank was put in, the washrooms were improved, the parking lot was paved, wheelchair access walkways were installed, electric and phone lines were buried and roadway lighting was erected. As expected, not everyone was happy with the modernization, but if Peggy's Cove was going to host the throngs of tourists who made the pilgrimage there each year, accommodations would have to be made.

With each tourist season, the numbers of visitors continued to grow. More and more bus tours and cruise ships coming to Halifax were putting Peggy's Cove on the itinerary. Deborah Jones, reporting in the Toronto *Globe and Mail*, said that the Sou'Wester was serving over 250,000 people per year. Some life-long residents of the area were feeling unhappy with the annual invasion and the inherent commercialism that it brought to a once-quiet village. Not everyone in town wanted to prettify their home or fish shack to satisfy the camera-toting hordes who were looking for that perfect seaside image to show their relatives back home.

As well, there were safety issues to be addressed. The Halifax *Chronicle-Herald* reported that the only rescue equipment on the rocks was a single life buoy on a rope posted at the lighthouse. Despite the potential for more tourists being swept out to their deaths, no level of government seemed willing to take any responsibility. The Coast Guard said it was not their problem and the province was not willing to step in and take any measures to protect the visitors to the Cove, despite the fact that those very tourists were bringing significant dollars into the province. And it was clear that if there was a single destination high on the list of most people coming to Nova Scotia, it was Peggy's Cove.

11

A Sea of Peril

WARNING
* Stay away from the water's edge
* Avoid wet or dark coloured rocks
* Stay far back during high winds
  and rough seas

A clear message on a cold day.

A gain in December of 1990, the waves of Peggy's Cove pulled another victim into the cold, deadly waters. A man was knocked down by a wave and swept from the rocks as his three small children and his wife looked on. A retired Halifax firefighter named Norman Stone was on hand. He ran to his truck, grabbed a rope and was able to toss one end to the victim, who struggled to stay afloat yet was unable to pull himself back up onto the slippery granite. Stone hauled the man ashore and, with some assistance, got him to the Sou'Wester, where he received first aid. Afterwards, the man's wife drove him to Victoria General Hospital in Halifax. Stone, who had recovered from a broken back seven years before and had undergone a spinal tap just two days before this incident, had been the right man at the right time to avert what could have been another tragedy.

Undoubtedly, there have been dozens of close calls on the rocks – most of them unrecorded. In 1994, from mid-May to mid-October, two safety patrollers in the employ of the province monitored the situation on the rocks. Rescue equipment was improved to some degree and more signs were added, for a total of sixteen, warning of the dangers.

In recent years, cold weather no longer deterred visitors from the scenic wonders of Peggy's Cove. On Sunday, February 5, 1995, sightseers headed to the rocks after hurricane-force winds had generated giant waves that were sending sea spray fifty feet into the air. Twenty-eight-year-old dental hygienist Andrea Clare Brennan and her friend, Barry Puto, were among those who drove out to watch the spectacle. They were standing not far from the lighthouse on what normally would have been a place that was high and dry when a gigantic wave slammed ashore, overtaking them and carrying Andrea towards the sea. Barry tried to grab her but, in doing so, slipped and fell off a ledge, falling four metres and breaking his leg.

Peter McLaughlin of the Halifax *Daily News* reported that Pascal Routledge and Joe Flinn witnessed the events from the parking lot of the Sou'Wester and they rushed to help. Routledge told the reporter, "I grabbed him [Barry Puto] by the scruff of the neck and back of the pants and dragged and half-threw him up onto the rock where Joe was. Puto screamed, "Look for her, look for her!" But no one left on the rocks could see the woman who had been washed into the killer waves.

The Coast Guard was called and attempts were made to launch the rescue craft, *Sambro*, but it could not leave Sambro Harbour due to the high seas. Seventy-eight-year-old Weldon Publicover, who lived in West Dover just down the shore from Peggy's Cove, said the storm had produced the worst waves he'd seen in seventy years. A Labrador helicopter was dispatched from CFB Greenwood and searched the area east of the rocks with searchlights from 6:30 to 9:30 that evening without success. It is unlikely Andrea would have survived very long with the water temperature just slightly above freezing.

Ever a place of mystery, Peggy's Cove found itself in the headlines yet again in 1995, but this time for a rather curious reason. In July of that year, Wallace Hubley of Seabright found a boulder in the barrens with three iron pegs beneath it. It weighed well over a hundred tons and was seven metres long, three metres wide and nearly three metres high. The boulder was covered with lichen and moss as usual but here it was sitting on three cubed "legs," each ten centimetres long. Who or what could have created this odd phenomenon? Hubley told the newspapers that he wondered if it could be some clue to hidden pirate treasure or some kind of massive ancient memorial to the dead. It was a true puzzle that got people talking about even wilder possibilities.

Scrapings from the cubes were analyzed at the Technical University of Nova Scotia and found to be 84 percent iron but the dating of creation was uncertain. No one had a clue as to how the odd rock monument came into existence.

The next day, however, John Little, a charming, brilliant and eccentric blacksmith and metal artist from nearby East Dover, came forward with the explanation. Little said that in 1985 he had "created" this piece of rock art as a tribute to a former NSCAD student of his, Dion Kilner, who had proposed putting "legs on stone." Little had created the monument himself with some help involving a twenty-ton hydraulic jack and a bulldozer, lifting and positioning the rock on the square legs to create this wilderness work of art. Thus the mystery was solved.

Swissair Flight 111 was referred to by some as the "U.N. shuttle" since so many United Nations officials travelled on it. On September 2, 1998, the McDonnell Douglas MD-11 was on a scheduled flight from New York's JFK Airport to Zurich, Switzerland, when electrical problems caused the pilot to prepare for an emergency landing at Halifax International Airport. The pilot took the jet in a wide arc out to sea in an attempt to dump excess fuel in preparation for the event. The plane was out over St. Margaret's Bay, thirteen kilometres from Peggy's Cove, when a near complete electrical failure caused the pilot to lose control of the huge aircraft. It smashed into the waters of the bay and all 229 people on the plane died, probably upon impact.

The trouble had begun at 10:10 p.m. when Captain Urs Zimmerman and First Officer Stephen Loew noticed smoke in the air conditioning vents. The smoke increased and within a few minutes a "pan-pan" emergency signal was sent out. The crew put on oxygen masks and began descending as they proceeded with the proscribed emergency procedures. But by 10:24, the flight instruments and auto-pilot began to fail. Investigators would later learn that the problem began with overheating of the entertainment system and faulty wiring with flammable sheathing. This combination is what led to the fire. Other flammable materials in the structure allowed the fire to spread, ultimately bringing down the plane.

If the pilot and his copilot had been able to control the

plane for eight to ten more minutes, they likely could have landed it at the airport, but the loss of power was so devastating that there were probably no last-minute efforts that could have saved the passengers. The plane broke apart as it hit the surface of the water and began to sink to a depth of fifty-five metres.

Most Peggy's Cove residents did not hear the plane overhead, but many went outside when they heard something – an explosion, or thunder, some thought, but it was the sound of the impact of the plane hitting the bay at 10:30 p.m. Soon after, sirens were heard coming from the firehouse and fishermen from around the bay took to their boats, heading out into the now quiet, dark night to look for survivors.

Nova Scotia emergency rescue organizations leaped into action. Search aircraft arrived, as did Maritime Command search-and-rescue boats. Official and unofficial would-be rescuers worked through the night and into the morning and well beyond, scouring a seventy-eight-square kilometre region. People from many communities around the bay volunteered, opening their homes and offering food to the searchers. Volunteers and professionals saw some horrific sights as body parts and wreckage from the plane surfaced and were taken aboard the boats. Many who helped out that night were traumatized by what they saw and were troubled by nightmares long after.

In the days that followed, as the rescue mission became a recovery mission, the media from around the world descended upon Peggy's Cove and made life almost unbearable for those who lived there. It seemed that TV, radio and newspaper reporters wanted to interview anyone they could find to squeeze some tidbit of information from them concerning this horrendous tragedy.

Local residents remained generous, however, taking searchers into their homes for food and rest as many of them put in long hours to help in the search. *Maclean's* magazine would report what those search efforts would bring: "Only 'fragmented' human remains and personal effects." These included items "ranging from a sweater found floating on the oil-slicked water, to a Bible, a still-legible postcard of New York City, a necktie, children's toys, a handwritten diary and a birthday balloon."

More than 800 family members of the victims came to Halifax the next week and most made the sad pilgrimage to Peggy's Cove or a neighbouring community. Once again, people around the bay opened their homes to the visitors and offered transportation and food. One mother of four, Irene Hirtle from Tantallon, told reporter Cynthia Driskill, "I know what I would feel like if it was my family. I couldn't imagine a family going to an empty hotel room. They need someone to be there to listen, extend love, sympathy, compassion, or help with children." There was also an outpouring of support from people around the province for the families, many of whom developed a permanent bonding with the province and the citizens who tried to comfort them.

Stephen Kimber, in his book *Flight 111: The Tragedy of the Swissair Crash*, reports many unusual and touching incidents regarding the aftermath of the crash, including the fact that Lyn Romano of New York had her deceased husband's wedding band returned to her. It was miraculously found in the search.

Fingerprints, dental records and DNA testing were used to identify those who died that night. The cockpit voice recorder and data recorder were located by the HMCS *Okanagan* and retrieved by Navy divers. Unfortunately, both recorders had stopped working six minutes before impact. The recovery operation lasted until December of 1999 when 98 percent of the aircraft was retrieved along with 18,000 kilograms of debris from the cargo. The Transport Safety Board investigation cost $57 million Canadian and took over four years to complete.

The *National Post* would later report that more than $300 million dollars worth of diamonds and jewels went down in the flight. It was also believed that a $50 million Picasso painting was lost in the crash.

Two monuments were erected in memory of the Swissair victims. One was built on the rock formation known as the Whalesback about a kilometre from the Cove. The second memorial was built adjacent to Bayswater Provincial Park across St. Margaret's Bay. The remains of the victims are buried there.

Lawsuits ensued over the deaths of the passengers and, in 1999, Boeing, the plane's manufacturer, and Swissair offered the families compensation but it was rejected. Next, a lawsuit of nearly $20 billion was launched by the families directed at Swissair and Dupont, the manufacturer of the Mylar wire sheathing that had caught fire, but in 2002 a U.S. federal court ruled against the claim.

In 2000, several Swiss families hosted young people from around Peggy's Cove in Switzerland as a gesture of thanks for the kindness of the community. One of the organizers was Ian Shaw who, after the death of his

A monument at the Whalesback to those lost in the crash of Swissair 111. The inscription reads: "In memory of the 229 men, women and children who perished off these shores September 2, 1998. They have been joined to the sea and the sky. May they rest in peace."

daughter in the crash, moved from Switzerland to Nova Scotia.

On midnight of September 28, 2003, Hurricane Juan slammed ashore on Nova Scotia with deadly wind strength and surging tides. The path of the storm was due north, coming from the Atlantic directly over Halifax and damaging coastal villages for many kilometres both east and west. Sustained winds were as high as 150 kilometres per hour with gusts up to 176. Wave heights were between ten and twenty metres at sea and, combined with high tides, there was considerable coastal flooding.

Juan ripped roofs off houses, levelled spruce forests and knocked down power lines on its swath across the province. The storm claimed the lives of eight people and left hundreds of thousands without power, some for weeks. Fortunately, no lives were lost at Peggy's Cove but the village did sustain damage.

Even though the harbour opens up to the west, a series of giant waves swept into the community from the east, snaking up through a narrow valley, through the lowlands and then over the breakwater built in 1915. The very fact that a breakwater existed on the east side of the village suggests that major storms in the past had surged into the Cove from this direction. Residents Roger Crooks and John Campbell were watching and took shelter as the winds became dangerously high.

They reported a wall of water not unlike a tidal bore surging up the valley several times, travelling over 400 metres of land and rising nearly seven metres. No one was hurt or caught in the swirling maelstrom but it did wreak havoc. A garage was mangled and the foundation of one of the gift shops was undermined. A driveway was wrecked and the soil beneath part of the road was washed away. The Sou'Wester parking lot was flooded and large boulders were moved by the force of the wave. The beams of the government wharf were contorted by the powerful tug of the currents as well.

The Cove had probably not seen a storm this fierce since a great "August gale" came ashore in St. Margaret's Bay on August 22, 1893, with winds of 180 kilometres an hour. Although all damage from Juan was repaired, it is clear that this will not be the last storm to attack the tiny village. Climatologists claim that global weather change and the melting of the arctic ice cap will lead to higher than normal sea levels as well as more fierce tropical and northern storms for Nova Scotia in the not-so-distant future.

Epilogue:

The Danger and the Wonder

The lighthouse and a throng of tourists.

I confess that twenty-five years ago I was not a fan of Peggy's Cove. I'd seen the images too many times on postcards. I'd heard the tourists rave about it. It seemed that everyone who visited Nova Scotia would make the trip to Peggy's Cove and snap endless photos. Today, a Google search will provide you with hundreds if not thousands of digital images of the lighthouse and the rocks.

I had believed that Peggy's Cove had become a kind of cliché, Nova Scotia's version of Disney World or the Wal-Mart of tourist destinations. I believed it wasn't the real thing. So I stayed away. I sought my coastal pleasures elsewhere on less crowded shores.

But then something changed. I made a few trips from my home at Lawrencetown Beach on the Eastern Shore of Nova Scotia to see what it was like there on winter days. And it was thrilling. I recall days when the salty wind was so fierce and unforgiving that it felt like it was going to rip the skin off my face. I could barely open the car door. I could barely stand upright on the smooth, icy rocks. Tears would stream down my face from the harsh elements as I fought my way out towards the lighthouse. And I would not dare go anywhere near the edge of the sea, for fear that a sudden gust would topple me into the zero-degree water and sloshing waves whose salty spray was freezing on the stone, glazing it with a perfect clear veneer of ice.

On another winter day, it would be windless. My breath would hang like a small cloud with each exhalation. The air was still cold – well into the negative digits. And there was an invigorating smell of clean salt air and sea. The sky was a pavilion of blue. I had driven here because the waves at my home at Lawrencetown Beach were massive, chundering to these shores from a storm hundreds of kilometres away, heading beyond Newfoundland and on towards Iceland. As soon as I woke up, I wanted to see what the waves were doing at the Cove. I was pretty sure the show would be impressive.

It was early on a Sunday morning and the parking lot was empty. The rocks were dry and ice-free as I walked towards the sea. Great plumes of white vaulted towards the heavens as the giant waves slammed into the coast. I walked the perimeter of the shoreline around the lighthouse, well back from the surging sea. As someone who surfs year-round in the North Atlantic, I am well aware of the terrible power of what a winter wave can do to a mere mortal. And I understand more than most how painful the cold of a winter sea can be. I surf in a dry suit in the frigid conditions of winter but once the zipper broke on my suit and when I fell off a wave, the freezing water filled the suit. It felt like knives stabbing me. I was weighted down by the water but able to get back onto my board and paddle ashore, then stumble towards my car and safety as the saltwater froze on my hair, creating long, elegant icicles. But I will never forget what it feels like to be immersed in zero-degree saltwater. So the danger signs at Peggy's Cove are heeded by this winter adventurer.

The thunder of waves like this on a windless day is a sound that fills the listener with awe. It is a deep and melodious tone that is felt inside the chest. It lets you know that you are in the presence of something powerful, something immense. You know immediately why the sailors and fishermen of the past had both admiration for and fear of the sea. The sound of those waves would haunt me long after I left that day. I was alone on the rocks and made my peace with Peggy's Cove. I realized that no matter how many tourists arrived, no matter how many tour buses filled with foreign visitors, no matter how many postcards and images were posted on the Internet ... I was sure now that Peggy's Cove would always be Peggy's Cove. The power of the place would not be diminished no matter what the future may bring.

Fast-forward to an early August day. It was bright and warm on the drive from Halifax all the way to West Dover and then the grey curtain of fog was visible off to the left. By the time I took the turn-off into the Cove, the fog was thick and heavy – a veritable cloud sitting on the land. But I had my backpack with my lunch and my notebook. I'd walk the rocks east of the Cove as planned and discover what there was to discover.

The Sou'Wester was preparing for a busy lunch crowd. The tour buses were parked neatly in rows. A string of Harley-Davidsons was arranged near the edge of the barrens. The license plates on the cars were from at least six provinces and five states. A parade of visitors was moving to and from the lighthouse, whose top was concealed by the fog. It was relatively quiet, the fog subduing the crowds in some inexplicable way. And there was bagpipe music drifting my way. I recognized the Scottish tune – "Dark Island," beautiful, sad and wondrous all at once. It was being played by a lovely woman in a kilt.

And then the fog began to lift, almost imperceptibly at first, but then a warm puff of a northerly land breeze began to usher the fog back to sea. I headed out onto the rocks and found one of those comfortable rounded formations that looked like someone had sculpted a seat for relaxing in the now-warm summer air. I took a sandwich out of my backpack and took my first bite, only to be smacked in the head with something that I thought was a rock. A split second later a rather large grey and white sea gull grabbed my sandwich and, in doing so, swatted me on the head with its wings. Some other visitors nearby looked on in astonishment and wondered if I was okay. Although I was not injured, I was shocked and angry that the gull, not me, got to eat my lunch. He must have gulped it down in one motion because he was now circling me, hoping to have a crack at the second half of my lunch but I wasn't going to give him the license. After a couple of threatening swoops, he flew to the roof of the Sou'Wester and seemed quite proud of himself.

Through years of living along the Nova Scotia coast, I had never seen a gull quite that brazen and I understood that it was the result of what was happening here at Peggy's Cove with such an influx of tourists. Although the continued increase of tourists would not alter the rocks or the sea, nor could it change the community much more from what it was now, it was clear that some of the natural

Boats afloat in the Cove.

elements of the area were changing. The largest of the gulls had lost their fear of humans and were now willing to pirate what they could from any unwary picnicker. It was not a comfortable fit. There would be other changes and challenges ahead.

Fresh water at Peggy's Cove had always been a problem for residents. There was not enough drinking water at the Sou'Wester for all the needs of the restaurant and the restrooms. Tanker trucks were now needed to haul in water on a daily basis through the summer months and beyond. Sophisticated waste disposal systems were necessary to prevent pollution, the most interesting being the composting toilet system at the nearby information bureau.

Having recovered my composure from the sea gull attack, I took a quick stroll around the tiny harbour and saw a handful of fishing boats still moored in the water. Several older boats were high and dry, some of them already beginning to rot and left there, not as eyesores, but as photogenic remnants of the days gone by. There was a healthy trade going in the many shops but little sign of traditional Cove activities except for some fishermen drying their nets on bare rocks across the road from the deGarthe monument.

I walked into the yard of the gallery and up close to the carved granite wall that William deGarthe had created. I studied the carvings in the rocks, trying to imagine the hundreds of hours that went into such a difficult task and thankful that my art involved words and not chisels.

A recently installed placard near the road offered tidbits of natural history, including details about glaciers, flora and fauna. Most interesting was the news that the bright orange lichen that grew like primitive fungal flowers on the rocks survived thanks to the nutrients provided by the droppings of sea gulls like the one who had stolen my sandwich. My lunch would go straight into the food chain that was an integral part of the living system of this place.

An hour later, I leave the crowds behind and walk east – up and down and around the great formations of granite by the shore, listening to the bagpipes fading in the distance. It doesn't take long, even on the most crowded day, to leave civilization behind at the Cove.

I sit down on an isolated ledge, my back to the boulder behind me and before me the soft pull and tug of the summer sea. Sitting here, alone, I feel like I am a million miles from anywhere and realize again that there is still peace to be found here in this intimate rendezvous with the rocks and the sea. Not far from where I sit are patches of that orange lichen, healthy and bright in the summer sun. I am reminded of what Bill Bryson had to say about lichen in his *A Short History of Nearly Everything*: "They are just about the hardiest living organisms on earth." Lichen grow in impossible locations on barren rocks. Bryson points out that it can take fifty years for lichen "to attain the size of a shirt button." The lichen here are as large as saucers. How many seasons have they endured?

There are steep drop-offs nearby and glacial grooves and etchings that look like artwork left by the Ice Age. There are multiple crevices to jump across and deep clefts, as well as small round holes that seem to have been drilled in the stone.

Back away from the shoreline, there are pools of clear standing water and small pockets of soil where moss grows along with a few small colourful flowers, including some blooming wild irises and dwarf roses. There are few birds here today, although it is not uncommon to observe cormorants and other sea ducks of many varieties in the waters beyond the shore. Of course, there are many varieties of gulls, shearwaters and other sea birds that swoop and skim above the waves.

In the small inlet east of the Cove, the kelp and other seaweed undulate back and forth – a rich array of colours – green and brown and bright rust colours. Eelgrass has washed up and is drying in the sun in the low marshy area among the sea rocket, glasswort and orach. Here sparrows sway on the stalks of sea oats and remain wary of both intrusive humans like me and the hawks that pass over on a regular basis.

Eelgrass, despite its fairly mundane presence as a long flat filament, is a vital part of the food chain. Officially known as *Zostera marina*, it is not a true seaweed but a perennial flowering plant that grows in subtidal zones such as this. Eelgrass does a worthy job of filtering pollutants from the water. It provides shelter for tiny crabs and lobsters and is a source of food for many species. The blades of living eelgrass are solar collectors that have the capacity to produce oxygen. Eelgrass can survive and thrive in mere centimetres of water or at depths of more than thirty feet.

When it is uprooted and begins to decay, it sustains bacteria, worms and crabs that support higher levels of life. Nutrients from eelgrass help to feed scallops, lobsters, flounder, mussels and other sea life. Ducks and other waterfowl frequently feed in these beds because of the rich diversity of life supported by eelgrass.

In years gone by, eelgrass was used for packaging,

A lone hiker on the polished rocks.

bedding and for insulation in the walls of houses. Today, residents of Peggy's Cove continue to use dried eelgrass for mulching and composting in their gardens. And a single pile of eelgrass in the backyard is a good place to grow soilless white, yellow, blue and red potatoes.

Not far from the inlet, in small pockets of wet soil, more irises bloom, and delicate orchids can be found growing in wind-protected pocket marshes. They have names like Grasspink, Dragon's Mouth and Ragged Fringed Orchid and it is hard to believe that such elegant, delicate flowers could survive in such a difficult place. Pitcher plants and sundew flytraps grow in the marshes as well, capturing live insects and consuming them for sustenance.

And I am reminded that the granite beneath my feet

Some of the houses of the village with the church in the background.

was glowing molten liquid 370 million years ago and that much later the rock here was scraped and gouged and ultimately polished by the glaciers in both their advance and retreat. Those surreal-looking boulders to the north that sit strangely positioned atop the bedrock, as if scattered by giants, are known as glacial erratics and were left here along the coast and in the barrens by the melting glaciers.

I stop to lean up against a sun-drenched wall of rock and put my cheek to it, feeling the warmth the summer sun stored in the stone. At this moment, I feel like I have been transported a million years into the past. That's what Peggy's Cove can do. If you give it a chance, it can take you out of yourself and the world you live in and deliver you to a place that is both profound and enduring.

In 2001, the census recorded the resident population of Peggy's Cove as fifty. The recent monument greeting travellers at the turn-off into the Cove states it is now forty. In 1989, the province of Nova Scotia estimated that over 120,000 tourists a year visited Peggy's Cove. My guess is that the number has doubled since then. Such a ratio of tourists to residents is more than a little daunting. And some might wonder how anything authentic can remain in such a place.

But as I turn to walk back towards the lighthouse, the throngs of tourists and the carnival atmosphere of the paved parking lot, I realize that the yearly invasion of travellers will not diminish this place. What is real here is still very real. Peggy's Cove is a place of both danger and wonder that will endure for generations to come.

Bibliography

Atlantic Geoscience Society. *The Last Billion Years: A Geological History of the Maritime Provinces of Canada.* Halifax, Nova Scotia: Nimbus Publishing, 2001.

Baird, David. *Northern Lights: Lighthouses of Canada.* Toronto: Lynx Images Inc., 1999.

Beck, J. Murray. *Joseph Howe: Voice of Nova Scotia.* Toronto: McClelland and Stewart, 1964.

Bird, Will R. *Off-Trail in Nova Scotia.* Toronto: McGraw-Hill Ryerson, 1956.

Boutilier, Mrs. Walter H. "A Bluenose Veteran Over Eighty Years." Unsourced newspaper clipping from February 10, 1924. Found in the PANS scrapbook on Halifax Districts at Nova Scotia Archives. MG9 vol. 43 (microfilm #15090) p. 375.

Bowyer, Peter. "Hurricane Juan Summary." Environment Canada. October 29, 2003. http://www.atl.ec.gc.ca/weather/hurricance/juan/summary_e.html

Brooks, Patricia. "An Omission in Peggy's Cove Commission: Residents call for government to fill positions." *Sunday Herald.* 13 Dec. 1998.

Choyce, Lesley. *Nova Scotia: Shaped by the Sea.* East Lawrencetown, Nova Scotia: Pottersfield Press, 2007.

Creighton, Helen. *Bluenose Magic.* Toronto: McGraw-Hill Ryerson Ltd., 1968.

Croft, Clary. *Chocolates, Tattoos & Mayflowers.* Halifax, Nova Scotia: Nimbus Publishing, 1995.

deGarthe, William E. *This is Peggy's Cove, Nova Scotia, Canada*. Self-published: 1956.

Davis, Bob. "Peggy's Cove." *Evening Mail*. 30 Aug. 1934: 4.

Doane, Frank A. *Nova Scotia Sketches*. Truro, Nova Scotia: Truro Printing and Publishing, 1949.

Duffy, Peter. "Development Feud Builds at Peggy's: $610,000-project splits Cove." *Mail Star*. 22 July 1988.

Driskill, Cynthia. *Maclean's*. 14 Sept. 1998: 20.

"Experts Scratch Heads as They View Strange Sea Monster: Horned Sea Beast Captured at N.S. Fishing Village is Puzzle." *Chronicle*. 9 Feb. 1940: 40.

"Father, Son Swept to Death While Watching Storm." *Chronicle-Herald*. 6 Oct. 1962: 1, 5.

Fergusson, Bruce and William Pope. *Glimpses into Nova Scotia History*. Windsor, Nova Scotia: Lancelot Press, 1974.

Fisher, Robert C. "Within Sight of Shore: The Sinking of the HMCS *Esquimalt*, 16 April 1945." http://www.familyheritage.ca/Articles/esquimalt1.html

Forbes, Ernest. "Rum in the Maritimes' Economy During the Prohibition Era." *Tempered by Rum: Rum in the History of the Maritime Provinces*. Eds. Morrison, James H. and James Moreira. East Lawrencetown, Nova Scotia: Pottersfield Press, 1988. 103-110.

Hayes, Brian. "Patrollers Begin Rock Watch to Make Peggy's Cove Safer." *Chronicle-Herald*. 13 Apr. 1995.

Hines, Sherman. *Peggy's Cove Nova Scotia: Photographs by Sherman Hines*. Halifax, Nova Scotia: Nimbus Publishing, 1992.

"Insurer Wants to Look for Treasure in Swissair Debris: 'This is tasteless'." *National Post*. 19 May 2000: A8.

Irwin, E.H. Rip. *Lighthouses and Lights of Nova Scotia: The Complete Guide*. Halifax, Nova Scotia: Nimbus Publishing, 2003.

Jones, Deborah. "Tourism development creating dissension in Peggy's Cove." *The Globe and Mail*. 10 Oct. 1989.

Kimber, Stephen. *Flight 111: The Tragedy of the Swissair Crash*. Toronto: Seal Books, 1999.

Livesay, J.F.B. *Peggy's Cove*. Toronto: Ryerson Press, 1944.

Macleod, John. "The Dryness of the Liquor Dealer." *Tempered by Rum: Rum in the History of the Maritime Provinces*. Eds. Morrison, James H. and James Moreira, East Lawrencetown, Nova Scotia: Pottersfield Press, 1988. 76-87.

McLaughlin, Peter. "They Tried to Run." *Daily News*. 7 Feb. 1995: 3.

Mercer, Doug. "Peggy's Cove: Waves from the East?" Environment Canada. October 17, 2003. http://www.atl.ec.gc.ca/weather/hurricane/juan/peggys_cove_e.html

Moreira, James. "Rum in the Atlantic Provinces." *Tempered by Rum: Rum in the History of the Maritime Provinces*. Eds. Morrison, James H. and James Moreira. East Lawrencetown, Nova Scotia: Pottersfield Press, 1988. 15-29.

Nunn, Bruce. *History with a Twist: Unusual Stories from Mr. Nova Scotia Know-It-All Bruce Nunn*. Halifax, Nova Scotia: Nimbus Publishing, 1998.

O'Neill, Mora Dianne. *Paintings of Nova Scotia: from the collection of the Art Gallery of Nova Scotia*. Halifax, Nova Scotia: Nimbus Publishing, 2004.

Parsons, Robert C. *The Edge of Yesterday: Sea Disasters of Nova Scotia*. East Lawrencetown, Nova Scotia: Pottersfield Press, 2003.

"Peggy's Cove Saluted in Canada Post Series." *Mail Star*. 22 June, 2002.

"Peggy's Cove Still No.1" *Chronicle-Herald*. 6 July 1985.

Perry, Hattie A. *Old Days Old Ways: Early 20th Century Nova Scotia*. Tantallon, Nova Scotia: Four East Publications, 1989.

Peters, Tom. "On a Rocky Footing: Man hopes to unlock secret of boulder near Peggy's Cove." *Chronicle-Herald*. 27 Sept. 1995.

Peters, Tom. "Mystery Solved: Blacksmith pegged rock." *Chronicle-Herald*. 28 Sept. 1995.

Pope, Douglas. *deGarthe: His Life, Marine Art and Sculpture*. Hantsport, Nova Scotia: Lancelot Press, 1989.

Robinson, Parker. "Emergency at Cove Rapped." *Chronicle-Herald*. 3 Aug. 1990.

Rossiter, Jim. "Surf Sweeps Woman Away: Man washed back to rocks at blustery Peggy's Cove." *Daily News*. 6 Feb. 1995: 3.

Sampson, Anita M., Howard Donohoe and Martha Devanney. *A Walking Tour of Rocks, Minerals and Landforms of Peggy's Cove*. Information circular 9. Nova Scotia Department of Mines and Energy: March 1989.

Sclanders, Ian. "Seaside Shangri-La." *Maclean's Magazine*. 1 Aug. 1947: 12.

Shiers, Kelly and Heather Hueston. "Peggy's Cove Visitor Pulled From Waves." *Chronicle-Herald*. 13 Dec. 1993: A1.

SwissAir Flight 111 Memorial. http://www.waymarking/com/waymarks/WM2YVM

Illustrations and Photo Credits